AMY KENDRICK  'IN

table for two

Doing life and savoring
Scripture together

LifeWay Press®
Nashville, TN

ISBN: 9781415868416
Item Number: 005260394

Dewey Decimal Classification Number: 248.843
Subject Heading:
DISCIPLESHIP \ BIBLE—STUDY AND TEACHING \ GIRLS—RELIGIOUS LIFE

Printed in the United States of America

Student Ministry Publishing
LifeWay Church Resources
One LifeWay Plaza
Nashville, TN 37234-0174

We believe that the Bible has God for its author; salvation for its end;
and truth, without any mixture of error, for its matter and that all Scripture
is totally true and trustworthy. The 2000 statement of *The Baptist Faith
and Message* is our doctrinal guideline.

Unless otherwise indicated, all Scripture quotations are taken from the
Holman Christian Standard Bible® Copyright © 1999, 2000, 2002, 2003
by Holman Bible Publishers. Used by permission.

Verses marked NIV are from the Holy Bible, New International Version,
copyright © 1973, 1978, 1984 by International Bible Society.

contents

about the authors

Ministry was not simply a vocation but a lifestyle in the Kendrick house. Through travel and God's Word, God gave AMY KENDRICK PIERSON a heart for people all over—from leper colonies in Vietnam to villages in Romania. In 2007, she graduated from Southwestern Baptist Theological Seminary. Her studies brought growth, an internship with a church the size of a small town, and an introduction to Kyle, who became her husband. She now serves as girls' minister at Prestonwood Baptist Church in Plano, Texas. She loves being married to her amazing husband and loves counseling, discipling, and mentoring girls (three completely different things!).

Passionate is a word that is sometimes overused, but it fits MONA CORWIN. She lives in Texas and is married to her high school sweetheart, Warren. They're parents to five children, making their lives a whirlwind of laughter. Mona's passion is Jesus and seeing His Word ignited in the generation she has been called to serve. Mona takes the Titus 2 call seriously. After 15 years of teaching and speaking, she founded "Amazing Things Ministry" and is also the creator the Jesus Advent Tree.

ACKNOWLEDGEMENTS:

Amy: Kyle, my awesome hubby—in you, I see Christ. Thanks for telling me this book wouldn't forever live in my Mac. Mom and Dad—you rock an entire country for Jesus. You're my biggest heroes. Matt—you're my best friend and role model for contagious faith. Bec and JJ—one of the biggest thrills of my

life is seeing you walk by the Spirit. Richard and Gina—thanks for showing me the world. My family—you put Christ first and convinced me He could do anything through me. My community, buddies, student staff, and my girls and disciples—I'm blessed by unconditional love and cracking up . . . the church being the church.

Mona: Warren, my forever love—thank you for loving me like Christ loves the church. Life with you, the great adventure. My children: Brett, Mallory, Max, Molly, Andreza, and Stacie—I have no greater joy than seeing my children on fire for God. My unique family tree: Mom Barb, Uncle Tom, CJ, Uncle Randy, Rosie, and Joyce—your discipleship totally reflects the concepts of this book. My sisters in Christ: Karen, Susie, Cindy F, Cheryl, Titia, Monica, and all who sit with me—I savor our laughter and honesty; you are precious treasures.

Amy & Mona: Our God—You not only saved us, but You also choose to use us. Yours is the glory. LifeWay girls, Pam Gibbs, and Avery Photography—thanks!

foreward

"Will you disciple me?"

"Will you mentor me?"

"Can we meet and maybe you can show me how to read my Bible like you do?"

"Can you teach me how to hear from God?"

Here is the real question: Why is every female in our church asking us this? You picked up this book because either you are asking these questions or someone is asking them of you.

More common questions we get: "So, ya wrote a book? What is that all about?" Every time someone asks this, we feel conflicted. Are they asking because they are making conversation or because they can't believe we actually wrote a book? The truth is, we can't believe it either. We don't hold doctorates in English and creative writing, nor have we been waitressing for six years hoping someone would pick up the manuscript we left under the menu. We wrote a book because we heard a need—the need for a tool to teach girls how to feed on God's Word for themselves (instead of relying on a youth minister or girls' leader). And we heard the need for a tool to help girls—from age 12 to 92—connect with each other through God's Word.

We asked our Father to help us not just point out a problem but to be part of the solution. Well, He did, and here we all are on this journey together.

All the books we found for "mentoring" answered different questions, which seem to fall in the following categories:

"What should I wear?"

"Me and that dude, are we a pair?"

"I see my daughter's midriff; what a scare."

"We went down the aisle, and now he doesn't seem to give a care."

These books are helpful and give us great answers to our daily problems with dating, modesty, marriage, and a host of other issues. The problem is, when the next crisis hits, we are back in the bookstore staring at the Christian living section again. What if we could define our problem, find the solution in God's Word, and actually walk daily with Him in a discipleship friendship with another girl? That is the question we will answer for you in this book.

We are Mona and Amy, and yes, we wrote a book—not only for ourselves but for you too. Enjoy!

introduction

OUR HEART'S CRY

You have to understand something about us. We are the people who go to the grocery store to pick up one thing, and an hour later, we have counseled a stranger in the potato chip aisle whose marriage is falling apart. Or we've talked to a cashier whose daughter ran away. We are not "extra-anointed." We haven't unlocked some secret code in the Bible. We've pursued Christ by reading His Word. Years of experience taught us that there are promises, principles, and guidance available to us for every situation. And they're waiting for us in plain sight. Discovering those promises always brings wisdom and produces peace and great confidence in our God. Laughing, sharing, and learning from each other, we grow daily in our pursuit of God and His unique and individual plan for each of us. Our lives are not perfect, but they are full of adventure. They are truly the definition of abundant.

However, we noticed that many of the women and girls to whom we minister live lives that no one would label as abundant. When a situation or crisis arises in their lives, panic sets in. Frustrated or in hysterics, they call us (or stop us in the chip aisle) in a frantic search for an answer to their situation. We are always happy to help, but we usually leave with a sinking feeling that she'll be somewhat unprepared for the next dilemma that comes her way.

THE CRY OF A GENERATION

A common cry seems to be coming from women and girls. Women's and student ministries around the country will tell you the same thing: women and girls want to hear from God on their own. They long for the Word to talk back to them. They want to hear and know the still, small voice of the Lord speaking tenderly to them through His Word. They long to be able to hear personal revelation from God like the Christian leaders around them—be it a Sunday School teacher or famous Bible teacher. They long to obtain a wisdom that creates confidence in God's Word and His unwavering presence in their lives, no matter the current situation.

In previous years, many women were content to learn in a "sit still while I instill" teacher setting. They came for two hours, ate, watched a video, and filled in the workbook blanks—at least for a week or two. While studies like that take us straight to the Bible to drink deeply, do we meet a personal Jesus whose mercies are new to us as individuals, or do we acquire secondhand information about Him? Are we relying on someone else's encounter with God as our own?

Large groups love a book or video-driven study, but interacting with God's Word is so meaningful when it is coupled with a living, breathing mentor. What happens when our study is on Old Testament sacrifices that day instead of what's really on our hearts? Many times, we need someone to help us find Scripture about jealousy or sadness at not getting into a certain college or not landing our dream job at age 22.

THE CRY FOR CONNECTION

There is another part of this cry that surprised us. Our e-mail inbox is flooded with requests for personal discipleship and mentors who will teach a girl how to read her Bible. These requests, including those from mothers wanting to connect with their daughters spiritually, seem to resonate on everyone's hearts and are vocalized to church leadership all over the country. Everyone wants to laugh and have girly fun, but there is a deeper longing. They not only hunger to have meaningful interaction with God, but they also yearn to be connected with each other. They crave more than shallow small talk, gossip, and rehashing the previous night's reality show drama. A real connection is at the core of our desires. We believe this desire is ingrained in every woman.

TABLE FOR TWO IS BORN

God hears our cry; His Word alone contains our answer. John 17:17 proclaims this promise: "Sanctify them by the truth, your word is truth." God's Word will satisfy our cry for connection through the knitting of our hearts together as we engage in His Word. God's Word will satisfy the need for intimacy in our relationship with Him. The answer to every cry of our mind, heart, and soul is found in God's Word.

We recognized this hunger for God's voice and His Word, and we heard the cry of women longing for deep connection. So, we set out to create a Bible study tool that would give ladies of all ages the confidence to discover Truth and hear from Him in His precious Word, the Bible. We also wanted to create an environment for a sister connection, of any age combination, where mutual mentoring could flourish. It had to be easy to remember, and just like our own sister-connection, it had to be fun. And *Table for Two* was born.

chapter one

the sister connection

MUTUAL MENTORING

The desire for connection and mentoring was evident among women we listened to, but we didn't have a way to describe the trend we were seeing. We spent weeks mulling over the requests and the passions in our hearts. We encountered a new term for meeting this timeless need: *mutual mentoring*.

> **Mutual Mentoring** is defined as:
> • Allies who stand together in the Word of God, respecting and benefiting from the uniqueness that each person brings to the relationship.
> • Friends who encourage each other to pursue spacious lives, rich in God's purpose—lives that produce a godly femininity that is a sweet fragrance to the generation they are called to bless.
> • Sisters in Christ who are walking together, revealing the beauty of pure hearts. Each should reflect Him and His glory in their lives and relationships, ultimately leaving a legacy of strength and loving connection to the generation that follows.

You are the only one who can know who is the best connection for you. A sister who is 20 can grow with a sister who is 12. An older widow can grow with a young married woman. Sorority sisters can grow as they experience life away from home. A mother can grow with her own child.

"I have been reminded of your sincere faith, which first lived in your grandmother Lois and in your mother Eunice and, I am persuaded, now lives in you also."
—2 Timothy 1:5 (NIV)

Following the example of 2 Timothy 1:5, we are inspired by the heritage left to Timothy by his grandmother and mother. In her love for Christ, Lois discipled her daughter and taught her to fear and love God. Then, her daughter Eunice taught her son to fear and love God. Timothy grew up to be a godly man with a sincere faith because of these women's passion for the Lord and their desire to see their family know and love Jesus. You picked up this book because you are not content with only hearing about Jesus on Sunday morning. You want to hear from Jesus and tell others about His Word every day. Find a sister who wants the same thing, and you will have a perfect connection for mutual mentoring. That same legacy that lived in Timothy's family can be born in your own life.

iron sharpens iron

The kind of relationship reflected between Lois and Eunice is not bossy or condescending. It lifts up, encourages, and brings joy. Don't you long for friendships like that? Many of our relationships are condemning, hurtful, or distant. Let's take a fresh look at Proverbs 27:17 as our goal: "Iron sharpens iron, and one man sharpens another."

Women become a strong force when they work together as allies and not enemies. They are no longer competitors but friends when they view each other as uniquely designed parts of the body of Christ. Sisters who sharpen each other not only bless others but also receive blessing. The result of mutual mentoring will be a woman who will:

- Cross generational lines to teach another woman to become all that Christ created her to be in Him.
- Be trustworthy with information given and vulnerable in sharing information.
- Laugh.
- Cherish and respect others as equally precious in the eyes of God.
- Make an impact on the world around them as God created them to.

leaving a legacy

The Bible is filled with stories of faithful women who left godly legacies. Consider Ruth and Naomi. If Naomi had not radiated the love of God or modeled it to her daughter-in-law, Ruth would not have followed Naomi's God and become one of God's people, integral to His plan.

He renews my life;
He leads me along
the right paths for
His name's sake.
—Psalm 23:3

Younger women need wisdom and godly counsel. They are bombarded by a godless culture telling them to sell out their bodies, minds, and souls for elusive perfection and a false sense of worth. Now is the time to reclaim and restore the minds and hearts of our sisters in Christ. Our duty is to impart the riches of Christ's grace by unlocking the power of God's Word. Our counsel will put a bandage on a problem. However, God's Word alone can heal a wounded soul and a disillusioned heart.

At the same time, older women need to recognize that as they mature and God works in their lives, they have a responsibility to invest in the lives of those younger than them, helping raise up the next generation.

As a child of God, you receive much: spiritual gifts, fruit of the Spirit, and earthly talents. You did not do anything to inherit these blessings; they are given simply because God is a Father who longs to bless you. However, you must choose what you will pass along to the next generation. Simply put: You receive an inheritance, but you leave a legacy. What kind of legacy are you leaving?

answer the cry

The time has come to proclaim how God's power is established when His Word is read, revealed, and reflected in our lives. Let us be the answer to a generation longing to learn God's Word, hear His voice, and see victory in life. Let's become like Ruth, Naomi, Lois, or Eunice and establish a long line of Christian followers so rooted in sound doctrine and unwavering faith that they cannot be deceived by every new philosophy or empty promise the world throws at them.

now don't you start crying

You have a purpose—to pass faith on to others. God has a perfect plan to make that happen! In this study there is not one teacher and one student or one leader and one follower. The Holy Spirit is your teacher, and both of you will provide encouragement, sharpening, and accountability to each other. In addition, we will walk you step by step through this process of growing in faith together. After we explain each step, we will work through a sample section (in chapters 3–7) with the two opposing topics "impossible" and "possible." After seeing this simple process, you can try it out for yourself. You'll find that it's pretty easy to follow, but the benefits are amazing!

Before you start, there are three things you need to determine: your sister, your place, and your time.

■ PICK A SISTER:

Get alone with God and ask Him these questions: *Am I a sister who's ready to sharpen someone else by encouraging her and speaking truth in love? Can I prepare my heart to yield to the Holy Spirit and allow Him to clean up my life? Am I prepared to mutually mentor someone else? Am I willing to rely on God in sweet submission?* Then, ask Him to show you whom He has already prepared for you to accompany on this journey. Pair up with someone who longs to know how to love God better by finding out how to hear Him speaking tenderly through His Word. Find a sister who isn't simply looking for girl talk over coffee but is seeking truth and accountability.

■ PICK A PLACE:

Place for God: You will be spending time alone with God in His Word four days each week. Pick a place that is quiet and comfortable, but not too quiet and comfortable (like 6 a.m. under your down comforter). Be sure to choose a safe place where wandering eyes can't read your journal, puppies can't chew up notes, and you aren't messing up an entire room the whole family uses. We suggest not taking over the den because you will certainly have to move your books for the Tuesday night Rock Band™ session.

And if somebody overpowers one person, two can resist him. A cord of three strands is not easily broken.
—Ecclesiates 4:12

Place for each other: One day each week, you'll be sharing with your sister what the Holy Spirit has taught you. We've given a detailed outline you can walk through on each "Sister Day," which includes questions, activities, and ways to serve each other. Make sure the place you meet is quiet with few distractions.

■ PICK A TIME:

Time with God: We suggest spending 30 minutes with God each morning. Throughout the Bible we see examples of people who spent time with God in the morning.[1] Trust us, it works.

AMY:

One morning I decided to skip my quiet time at the dining room table and instead spend that time with Him at the office. What did I do? I checked one e-mail as I flipped to Acts. Before I knew it, I'd spent ten minutes checking my e-mail. I read a verse in Acts and remembered that I was supposed to mail something the day before. I found the letter and a stamp, and then my 9 a.m. appointment showed up ten minutes early. So, I said I'd read my Bible on my lunch break, which we all know would never happen. I wonder how many situations frustrated me that day while God was thinking, *Amy, I had your answer for that, but where were you this morning?*

Your time with the Lord must be holy and set apart for Him so you can hear Him clearly. If you spend time with the Lord, you will find you can get so much more done.

Time together: Your sister needs to know that she is a priority to you, and you show her that by meeting weekly at a set time. Do not wait until the night before to set up a time to meet with each other. Schedule a week in advance, or set a fixed time for the full six weeks, such as every Tuesday at 4 p.m. We meet at 7 a.m., before we go to work and school. We do not have to compete with overtime at work, homework, or carpools. Our only conflict this early is our beauty sleep. But when we hear from God, our faces usually look less frantic anyway.

"Very early in the morning, while it was still dark, He got up, went out, and made His way to a deserted place. And He was praying there."
—Mark 1:35

"Let me experience Your faithful love in the morning, for I trust in You. Reveal to me the way I should go, because I long for You."
—Psalm 143:8

1. Who chose the morning?
• Abraham (Gen. 19:27)
• Hannah (1 Sam. 1:19)
• David (Ps. 5:3)
• Crowds (Luke 21:38)
• Jesus (John 8:2)

chapter two

the process

"I'm sorry, Mrs. Jones, but the test came back positive."
"Honey, I was cleaning Zach's room and found drugs."
"Rebecca, how will I ever get over this depression and find joy?"
"Jessica, I have to get rid of this bitterness."

Statements just like these are heard all over the world every day. People in desperate situations cry out for answers, are paralyzed by pain or crises, and wonder where to go and what to do for the answers they need.

You have probably been told that God's Word can help you in your time of need. But, when you are faced with something difficult, do you go to your Bible and find Scripture needed for dealing with illness, a son's rebellion, a money crisis, or finding the forgiveness that will set you free? Or are you frozen in panic and unable to find your Bible, much less a pertinent Scripture?

When we ask Christ to be our Savior, we are immediately and forever saved. I am not more saved than my pastor or vice versa. However, learning something new about God is a process that takes time and commitment. Some women may be more Christlike than their friends, and a 10-year-old sister may be able to find a Bible verse on anger faster than her college-aged sister. Some girls commit more wholeheartedly to the growing process and experience freedom in Christ because they know Him.

Memorize the short description given below. The next time a problem or crisis comes up, you'll head for your Bible and think:

1-2-3-4, God's Word has the answers I'm looking for.

"1"—Focus on three Scriptures
"2"—Find the definition
"3"—Fill in the Scripture
"4"—Follow the P's

When you learn how to approach Bible study using these simple tools, your confidence will rise knowing that as you look to Him and pursue His Word, you will be fully equipped to handle whatever comes your way.

Supplies for this process include:

• Sister
• Place

- Time
- Study Bible
- Web site with different Bible translations
- Study pages from this book (of course)
- English dictionary or Web site (such as *www.dictionary.com*)
- Greek and Hebrew dictionary(ies)

(We suggest Vine's for a hard copy or *www.blueletterbible.org*.)

As you learn how to use these study tools, you will find the truth, and the truth will set you free (John 8:32). This approach to studying God's Word always starts with a desire for answers. What are you looking for in your life? Do you have a desperate situation, or do you just want to know what God's Word says about bitterness? It all starts the same way—wanting to hear a word from God.

why study two topics?

We study two opposing topics for the one problem or question we're dealing with for a very special reason. Many times in our lives (and by many times, I mean every day), we need to renew our minds (Rom. 12:2) and take thoughts captive (2 Cor. 10:5). We need to identify the lie in our lives and remove it. A lie is anything that is unholy or not of God. Its great to find a lie and even to remove it from our minds. But if we want to renew our minds we must put something in the place of that lie. So, as we deny the lie and believe only the truth of what God says about it, we find victory. Consider the following:

A teenage girl develops an eating disorder because she believes the lie that she must look a certain way instead of believing the truth that she is perfectly created in God's image (Gen. 1:27).

A college girl dates a non-Christian boy because she believes the lie that she can change him instead of the truth that his bad habits will lead her down a path away from the Lord (1 Cor. 15:33).

A young mom spends time visiting with her friends all day instead of spending time with her children. She believes the lie that she does not know the Bible well so others should spiritually raise her children. Instead, she should believe the truth that passing down faith to her kids is her highest calling and will give her much joy (3 John 1:4).

> *"Do not be conformed to this age, but be transformed by the renewing of your mind."*
> —Romans 12:2a

> *"We demolish arguments and every high-minded thing that is raised up against the knowledge of God, taking every thought captive to the obedience of Christ."*
> —2 Corinthians 10:4b-5

17

A lady who has walked with God for 60 years believes the lie that only younger people can serve God instead of the truth that she has wisdom to pass on to the generations after her (Ps. 71:18).

Studying opposite topics allows you to get wisdom. It exposes every lie and harmful way, so that you can remove it from your life. Then, you can choose to use and speak the positive knowledge of God's truth over your situation and change your life.

To fully understand something, you have to see it from both sides. When we open God's Word, study the opposites, and are exposed to the truth, we then have a choice: we can choose the way of life or the way of death. Studying Scripture makes the choices clear.

remove and replace

"Wisdom is supreme—so get wisdom. And whatever else you get, get understanding."
—Proverbs 4:7

Once you have successfully identified the lie, you can remove it. However, the battle is not won just yet. If you do not replace the negative with a positive, you will fight that same battle again another day. So, you must choose to replace the old, negative, sinful thing with the new, positive, godly thing. Victory is sure when you know God's best, choose it, and then stand on that promise. Now, that sounds like the wisdom Proverbs 4:7 is talking about.

Let's consider the topic of rebellion. For two days, you will study and understand rebellion. You'll find Scriptures from God that will help you tear down the rebellion, but the battle is only half over. God wants to remove the rebellion, but a different type of rebellion will creep back into your life if you leave a void. You need to replace that area in your heart with obedience. By searching out both sides of a topic, you are removing the filth and replacing it with truth and victory. Rebellion out; Christ-centered obedience in.

opposites attract

In our lives, we struggle with different sins that need to be removed and replaced with truth, promises, and blessings that are ours in Christ. For this next activity, there are two columns: negative and positive. We've filled in one for you on each side. Set a one-minute timer and see how many opposites you can complete. (Our favorite timer is the microwave, but make sure you set the select timer, not the cook mode.) Compare your work with your sister when you meet. Begin!

NEGATIVE	POSITIVE
1. Sad	1. *Happy*
2. *Dirty*	2. Clean
3. Rebellion	3. *Submission*
4. *Anxious*	4. Content
5. Betrayal	5. *True*
6. _____	6. Mercy
7. Confusion	7. _____
8. _____	8. Refuge
9. Lazy	9. *Ambitious*
10. _____	10. Patience
11. Fear	11. *Calm*
12. _____	12. Steadfast

pressing on toward the prize

The Bible tells us we are overcomers (1 John 5:4-5) and conquerors (Rom. 8:37). After taking the quiz above, did you realize how opposite opposites really are? The opposite of patience is not the excuse, "Well, I was created that way." It's impatience. The opposite of perseverance is not just, "Oops" or "Oh well, it wasn't worth the effort." It's laziness. Paul tells us to press on to the prize that has been laid before us (Phil. 3:13-14). To do anything less is the opposite of pressing on. In a society of mediocrity that gives medals to everyone from first place to "good effort," we sometimes do not live with the prize in mind. We get comfortable with just existing, but we have been called out for much more. We are called

"Because whatever has been born of God conquers the world. This is the victory that has conquered the world: our faith. And who is the one who conquers the world but the one who believes that Jesus is the Son of God?"
—1 John 5:4-5

"No, in all these things we are more than conquerors through him who loved us."
—Romans 8:37 (NIV)

to greater depths in our relationship with God; we are challenged to feed on spiritual meat instead of milk.

the importance of listening

"If anyone has ears to hear, he should listen!" Then He said to them, "Pay attention to what you hear. By the measure you use, it will be measured and added to you. For to the one who has, it will be given, and from the one who does not have, even what he has will be taken away." —Mark 4:23-25

What are we to be hearing? God's Word. We hear it when we study the Bible and pray. Studying God's Word equips us to go through a trial; it trains us to mutually mentor a sister; it gives us the skills to guide a child. The Bible builds our faith in God's ability to direct our path. Be confident that He is the One giving us the help we need.

the value of equipping

Timothy tells us why the Scriptures were given to us:

All Scripture is inspired by God and is profitable for teaching, for rebuking, for correcting, for training in righteousness, so that the man of God may be complete, equipped for every good work. —2 Timothy 3:16-17

To be trained in righteousness means that we are being trained to live the life Jesus died to give us. Training is something that takes place before the actual event.

For example, marathon trainers begin their regimen of preparation months in advance. They don't wait until a week before the big race to begin training. The same thing applies to Olympic athletes. They don't wake up one morning suddenly prepared for the competition. Their lives are centered around their goal.

The same applies for spiritual training. You can't just wake up one morning and say to yourself, "I'm spiritually prepared to live like Christ in a crazy, immoral world." It just doesn't work like that.

Don't wait until the pressure is on to figure out how to get help from the Word. Be well trained. Life's pressures and challenges don't go away. And they don't wait for an opportune time. Some say the Bible isn't relevant in today's world. We know you will find God's Word not only highly relevant but also life-changing.

When you study the Word, get understanding in an area, and allow that understanding to shape your thoughts and your actions, you will find a calm strength in your life that will help you live above daily pressures. You can go through a difficult time with peace and trust in God. You can face a new and challenging situation because you know where the Help lies to make it through. You've spent enough time in God's Word to know that no matter what you face, encountering God in Scripture can help you succeed and thrive.

chapter three

the "I"

FOCUSING ON THREE SCRIPTURES

Remember the chant you needed to learn? "1-2-3-4, God's Word has the answers I'm looking for"? In the next few chapters, we will explain these four steps. Then, for several weeks you will work through preassigned topics to help you practice the steps. Working through those topics will help you develop your Bible study skills, but there's an added benefit. As you meet together with your big sis or little sis to discuss the topic, you'll discover that you're not only growing closer to God, but you're also growing closer to each other.

MONA LAUGHS:

I have used this Bible study process while raising our kids. During a busy volleyball season, our daughter will sometimes ask to skip Sunday School and do one of these studies instead. She knows she can hear directly from God just like her Sunday School teacher can. I have also used it to discipline our children. Studying "lying" or "kindness" has sometimes done more than a wooden spoon on the backside ever could!

As we explore this simple but effective Bible study tool, we will reflect and guide you through the process with an example. We will be using the two opposing topics, "impossible" and "possible," to walk you through the study process.

the "1"

The "1" represents focusing on three Scriptures. (To remember, just think about the first thing you need to do when you face a new problem or a question—look through Scripture!) To find Scriptures that contain your word or topic, you will need to look it up in a concordance.

Your Bible may have a limited concordance in the back, so you might want to purchase one. Inexpensive paperback versions are available online or at your local bookstore, but if you really want to dig deep, consider *The Strongest NIV Exhaustive Concordance* (published by Zondervan). It provides a complete indexing of every appearance of every word in the NIV Bible, even listing all the "of"s.

Another option is the *Holman Christian Standard Bible Comprehensive Concordance of the Bible* (by B&H Publishers), which omits common words (like "of") but indexes all the others found in the Bible. You'll find it very helpful as you begin to dig into God's Word.

Strong's Exhaustive Concordance of the Bible (also known as "Strong's Concordance") contains a cross-reference of every word in the King James Version of the Bible. It provides the original words and definitions in the original Hebrew (Old Testament) and Greek (New Testament).

Many Web sites offer concordances available to use for free, such as *www.blueletterbible.org*. Simply type in your topic or key word, and a list of all the Scriptures that contain that word will be given.

MONA RECALLS:

For my study of impossible vs. possible, I visited the official Web site of the ESV Bible (English Standard Version). Under the search button, I typed in "impossible." I found three verses: Judges 6:5, Matthew 17:20, and Luke 1:37. But I was curious, "What did the other Bible versions say?" So, I looked in the Amplified Bible and King James Version (KJV). Did you know that there are lots of versions of the Bible? You can research them and find one that you like best.

Keep in mind, though, that some Bibles are actual translations of the original Scriptures in Hebrew and Greek. Others, though, like *The Living Bible* and *The Message*, are paraphrases. This means putting a translation into current terms or phrases for better understanding. While it is easier to read, you can't really study God's Word from a paraphrase.

TAKE YOUR TIME

Take some time and allow the Holy Spirit to spark your interest in a few passages. You will enjoy reading all the different verses sprinkled throughout the Bible that contain your topic. Choose three verses and write them word for word in the space provided on the worksheet. Circle or underline the one you want to focus on that day. You'll focus on three more Scriptures the next day, so don't feel like you have to choose between two really good ones. You can just go back the next day and pick up the other verse you really liked.

AMY REMEMBERS:

Every Scripture won't apply to your need or situation. I was looking up "impossible" and one of the Scriptures had to do with a camel count in Judges 6! Obviously, it didn't apply to my situation (I didn't need to count camels!), so I looked for another Scripture. God loves for us to enjoy Him and His Word. Just like Mona, I looked up the word in several translations.

Humor and joy are necessary on the road trip of finding truth together, even to the point of giggling and silent laughter.

The "1" will look like this:

DISCOVERY, DAY 1

TOPIC 1	TOPIC 2
IMPOSSIBLE	**POSSIBLE**

---

1. FOCUS ON THREE SCRIPTURES

Using a concordance, look up several Scriptures that contain Topic 1. Choose three verses that seem most interesting and applicable to you. Focus on those Scriptures, writing them word-for-word in the space provided below. Choose one to study by asking the Holy Spirit to show you which verse to study today. Circle or underline it.

Judges 6:5 (NIV)—"They came up with their livestock and their tents like swarms of locusts. It was impossible to count the men and their camels; they invaded the land to ravage it."

Luke 1:37—"For nothing will be impossible with God."

Hebrews 11:6—"And without faith it is impossible to please God, because anyone who comes to him must believe that he exists and that he rewards those who earnestly seek him."

Keep in mind that we didn't show you all of the work for one day. We just showed you what the part "1" would look like. The next few chapters will show you what the rest of a day's work will look like on the page. To get a more complete picture, you might want to check out a blank day, such as page 62. This might clear up any confusion.

a quick word about eisegesis

If the word above left you scratching your head, don't worry. It's not a word from Chemistry class. It's actually a theological term. Eisegesis (pronounced i-seh-jee-ses) just means that a person misinterprets a verse in such a way that the verse supports a person's own ideas, making the verse say something that it didn't. For example, during the Civil War, some people said that Scripture supported slavery. They quoted verses like Ephesians 6:5, which says, "Slaves, obey your earthly masters with respect and fear, and with sincerity of heart, just as you would obey Christ." Some slave owners were trying to justify their behavior by using Scripture.

So how does this apply to you? You don't own any slaves, but you may face the same temptation to bend Scripture so that it supports your own ideas, opinions, and viewpoints (like if you're arguing with your parents about something). It would be tempting to find verses that support your ideas, but that's not the purpose of Scripture. We conform our lives to God's Word, not the other way around. As you focus on Scripture, let the Bible speak for itself. Be willing to allow it to change your heart and mind. If you don't, then why would you study it?

chapter four

the "2"

FIND THE DEFINITION

There are many Web sites that have dictionaries on them (www. dictionary.com or http://1828. mshaffer.com).

The "2" is all about defining the topics. Throughout the week, you will be directed in this section to define your two topics. The first day, you will use the English dictionary and then a Greek or Hebrew dictionary the second day. **DO NOT PANIC.** You don't have to know a word of Greek or Hebrew or need to enroll in a Bible college. Many godly men and women have created resources to help us. You are about to learn a great study skill, and you will love it—we promise.

it's all greek to me

Learning the original Greek or Hebrew definition of a word can sometimes shed great light on the meaning of a Scripture. And it can give you great insight into the English language. For example, do you know where the word "dynamite comes from? It actually comes from the Greek word "dynamis", which means "power." Learning the Greek and Hebrew words may actually become a favorite part of your study. You do not want to skip this step, we promise!

greek fun: not an oxymoron

For this activity, you will look at the Greek word and guess which is the correct word in English. You might be surprised at how many you know.

1. The Greek word *charis* means:
   a. grace   b. peace   c. goat   d. change

2. The Greek word *Christos* means:
   a. joy   b. disciple   c. goat   d. anointed or Messiah

3. The Greek word *kosmos* means:
   a. world   b. kindness   c. goat   d. Kramer

4. The Greek word *agape* means:
   a. full   b. ravine   c. goat   d. unconditional love

5. Bonus: Hebrew word עז means:
   a. faithfulness   b. gentleness   c. goat   d. self control

How did you do? Check your answers in the right margin of this page. We tried to not let you fall back to "If I don't know the answer, I'll go with c." However, we feel confident that you got the bonus if you did that!

greek or hebrew?

So how do you know if you are supposed to look in the Greek or Hebrew dictionary for the definition of a word you're studying? Good question, and one that's easy to answer. If the Scripture you are looking up is from the Old Testament, then you use a Hebrew dictionary. If the Scripture is from the New Testament, you use a Greek dictionary.

dictionary of greek and hebrew

Some ladies shy away from looking up the Greek or Hebrew words because Greek or Hebrew words may use the same English word but can actually have more than ten meanings. Some people are worried about using the wrong definition and misinterpreting a verse. To make sure this doesn't happen, we suggest *Vine's Complete Expository Dictionary of Old Testament and New Testament Words.* The Hebrew dictionary is in the front of the book and the Greek Dictionary is in the back.

Using Vine's helps ensure that the definition matches your chosen verse because the Scriptures are listed with the definitions, so you know where to look.

AMY REMEMBERS:

One Sunday a pastor was preaching on the different definitions of love in the Bible. "See, agape is the kind of love you have for your friend," he said. My friend looked at me and said: "No way. Agape is unconditional love. This is the kind of love God has for us. I'm sure I heard a pastor preach that not too long ago." I laughed and turned away to listen. Next thing I knew, she had taken out her iPhone and checked *blueletterbible.org*, proudly showing me that agape is actually God's kind of love.

To use *The Blue Letter Bible* Web site, simply type your word in the search box provided, select the translation or "Version," and click on "Search." When the list of results is returned, read through to see which verse you want to study, then click the Scripture reference beside it. Now, click on the "C" beside your verse, which stands for *concordance.* When you do that, a new box appears. It lists each English word in that verse. Next to each word is the Strong's *Exhaustive Concordance* number. If you click on the Strong's number, the Web site will pull up the exact definition.

AMY RECALLS:

I have never taken a formal Greek or Hebrew class. My daily time with the Lord has never included reading Matthew in Greek for a few hours every morning. But, several papers I had to write in seminary required looking up words in the original biblical language. In the beginning it felt a little weird because I did not grow up with study books open on my desk while spending time with Jesus. But, as I broke down a topic for a paper and put in the word's original meaning, the Scriptures came alive for me. Don't worry. You aren't learning another language. You don't have to be intimidated by pronouncing or writing the Greek or Hebrew word. Remember that you are simply looking up definitions, not conjugating verbs like in high school Spanish class.

On day 1, you will be looking up the first topic in the English dictionary. On day 2, you'll look up topic 1 in a Hebrew or Greek dictionary. You'll repeat the same process on days 3 and 4, except you'll be examining the topic's opposite. For our example, we provided the Greek definition for impossible since we figured you could handle an English dictionary on your own. Be sure to make a note of where you found the definition in case you need it later.

The "2" will look like this:

2. FIND THE DEFINITION.

Find and write down the Hebrew or Greek definition for topic 1.

Luke 1:37- "Impossible"- Verb meaning void of power. (Found in Vine's, Page 321)

Remember, we have only shown you a slice of what a day's work looks like. Peek ahead to page 62 to see an entire's day study. Again, we highly recommend, challenge, urge, and encourage you to complete this step. While it may be tempting to skip this step because you think you already know the definition, you will be missing out. The Greek and Hebrew languages are rich with nuances of meaning (like the difference between love for your parents and love for ice cream). By taking the time to learn what the original writers intended when they used a certain word, you are discovering a treasure of sorts, a treasure that some people will never enjoy because they just read Scripture like they read a comic book—a nice pastime but one with little lasting impact.

chapter five

the " 3 "

FILL IN THE SCRIPTURE

The "3" is about amplifying the Scripture with the English, Greek, or Hebrew definition. The purpose of this activity is to insert the definition into the verse. This will provide a richer and deeper understanding of the Scripture.

For example, Luke 1:37 says, "For nothing will be impossible with God."

• On day 1, the day you will look up the English definition of Topic 1, substitute the word "impossible" for the English definition (which was "incapable of occurring"). Therefore, for step three on day 1, this verse could be understood to say:

"For nothing will be incapable of occurring with God."

• On day 2, the day you use the Greek or Hebrew dictionary, substitute the word "impossible" for the Greek definition (which was a verb meaning "void of power"). Therefore, for step three on day 2, this verse could be understood to say:

"For nothing will be void of power with God."

The "3" will look like this:

3. FILL IN THE SCRIPTURE.

Write your chosen Scripture again and replace the word or topic with the definition you found to amplify its meaning.

Luke 1:37- For nothing is impossible (void of power) with God.

(Again, remember that we are only showing you a slice of your work. Refer to page 62 to see what a whole day's worth of study looks like.) This step always reveals the promises and character of our loving God. When you put the definition in the place of the word, the meaning of the entire verse is amplified and sometimes clearer.

We also learned that *impossible* was a verb. Verbs show action. God's power is not still; it is active. He is actively fighting for you and guiding you step by step every day. The next time your friend says that she cannot overcome a circumstance, you can respond that Luke tells us that the power of Christ is actively making all things possible for those who rely on Him. Don't you just love the Word of God?

christianese defined

As Christians, sometimes we are guilty of speaking "Christianese." We toss around church words without really understanding their meaning. You're probably guilty of doing the same thing. Try to define these words before looking to any dictionary or Web site for help.

1. Glory of God:

2. Gospel:

3. Evangelism:

4. Holy:

5. Salvation:

6. Sin:

----

7. Hell:

----

8. Grace:

----

9. Christian:

----

10. Beatitude:

Refer to a dictionary and see how your definitions compare. It will also be fun to compare with your sister the first day you come together to see how well you can articulate words that have become Christianese.

AMY SHARES:

In our Sunday morning service, we have a small group time to discuss the lesson we heard. We were studying 2 Timothy 4:5, "But as for you, keep a clear head about everything, endure hardship, do the work of an evangelist, fulfill your ministry." I asked, "If we are supposed to do the work of an evangelist, what is an evangelist?" Awkward silence. "Come on girls, if we're going to know whether or not we're doing the work right, we need to know what an evangelist is." These sweet junior girls who had been in church their whole lives shrugged. The conversation went on like this:

Girl One: "Um, I guess we tell people about Jesus."
Me: "OK, what about Him? Here is a clue. What is the gospel?"
Girl Two: "I think I heard the answer to that in an apologetics class this
        semester. Um, that Jesus died."
Me: "YES! Why did He die?"
Girl 3: "He died so we could be forgiven and not go to hell."
Me: "YES! So, the gospel is that Christ died so that I could be forgiven and
        live. And if an evangelist tells people the gospel, then...."
Girl 2: "An evangelist is someone who shares the gospel with others so
        that all can know that Jesus died so we can live."

These girls, like all of us, can use these Christianese words in a sentence without really understanding what they mean. By studying God's Word for yourself, you will learn the meaning of words you've never completely understood. This will help you to know God more intimately (you become closer to a person once you understand what he or she is saying!) and know how to live for Him.

chapter six

the "4"

THE THREE Ps

People from the Bible cannot be summed up in one verse, so we must figure out what their lives were really like. In the fourth section—the Ps, you will be acting like a detective. You are not content to skim over verses because you want to get into the setting and context to understand all that God wants you to learn in the passage.

Remember *The Chronicles of Narnia?* Little Lucy Pevensie went into a wardrobe and realized she was in a completely different world that needed to be saved. She tried to tell her brothers and sister about what she experienced, but they smiled and probably thought her ramblings were the result of some food she had eaten too late the night before. However, when they went into the wardrobe themselves, they saw and experienced everything Lucy told them.

In this final step, you will have the opportunity to read the firsthand accounts of stories from Old Testament saints and hear promises from disciples who walked with Jesus. With an open mind and open heart, ask God to help you be an avid participant in the passage. You'll focus on the three Ps:

Peruse—Examine the details
Personalize—Apply the specifics
Pursue—Delight in God

You will PERUSE these passages like a detective, examining the details to make the passage come alive in your life. You will PERSONALIZE the verses to see what God is specifically telling you. You will be encouraged as you realize that the Holy Spirit is your teacher and is speaking a unique Word to you. The last "P" is PURSUE. We honestly could not think of a better word or concept to describe how awesome it is to realize that the God of the universe—the God who made the sun rise this morning, Jesus who loves us unconditionally, and the Holy Spirit who guides us to truth—has spoken uniquely to us and wants us to chase after Him. You will delight in God who left the Bible as your companion as you walk (or run!) with Him.

PERUSE: EXAMINE THE DETAILS

Do you know what "peruse" means? Don't worry—many people don't! To peruse means to pay attention to or examine something intently, paying attention to the details. This can apply to lots of things, like a coin collector looks closely at a coin or an antique dealer looks at the details of a piece she is appraising. The term "peruse" can also apply to something that you read, such as Scripture.

In this step, you will look closely at the facts and details within the passage that contains your verse. Take the Scripture you circled and ask God to let certain words and phrases stand out to you. Meditate on all the aspects of the account and the words or phrases that seemed to leap off the page to you. As you meditate on your verse, read the verses before and after, taking your time. Pay attention to the context of the passage. Get the big picture of what's going on.

MONA RECALLS:

One time someone asked me, "How long do you think about the Scripture and meditate on it?" I realized she was asking me how many minutes. I responded, "It's not about minutes; just keep meditating on it until that Scripture speaks to you...until you get an 'Ah Ha!' moment. God's Word is living, and it will talk to you." She called me back several days later and said she'd received an answer. She knew what changes needed to be made in her circumstance because she thought about the verses and let them simmer in her mind and heart until she got an answer. Interestingly, she never mentioned how many minutes it took.

PERUSE: START DIGGING

We want things easily and immediately. We are the "microwave generation." However, to peruse is not to glance flippantly. Many times in the Bible, we skim over a passage or reread our favorite psalms quickly because we are seeking a quick phrase or verse that applies to our lives without requiring any effort or understanding on our part. Questions 1 through 4 of this section in each day's study will help us get the background on the passage we're reading.

Knowing the setting can cause the story or the verses to come alive. For example, let's say your study brings you to the story of the woman at the well (John 4). If you simply write down that the story is taking place at a well, you miss that she went to the well in the heat of the day. Checking commentaries and notes from a study Bible tells you about the customs of the day: only women who were considered unworthy and undesirable went to the well at that hour. Suddenly, the setting makes the character come alive. The setting is not simply a well, but a place that shows how unwelcome this type of woman was among more "reputable" women.

The second set of questions addresses the overall plot and background: What was happening? Does the culture of that day play a role? If so, how? Many times a verse can be taken out of context if the reader only reads one sentence out of a chapter. Verses should be read and understood in the context of the story.

For example, let's say you only read Genesis 29:11, "Then Jacob kissed Rachel and wept loudly." You are feeling all mushy and excited about their great love for each other. Well, you should. They loved each other

---

MEDITATE: **to think deeply and carefully; to roll over and over in your mind; to consider a thing.**

If we were to meditate on Romans 12:2, we'd like to memorize it and ask questions about each word like:

• God, what does it mean to be transformed?

• Jesus, is there anything in my life that I'm conforming to?

• Holy Spirit, what thoughts of mine need to be renewed?

Ask for yourself as you think about each word.

deeply. But, if you peruse through all of chapter 29, you see that Rachel's father tricked Jacob into doing hard labor for seven years before and after he married Rachel (14 years of work!). The entire account must be read so the meaning of a single verse can be fully understood in the context of the overall plot.

Questions 5, 6, and 7 deal with the characters' role and interactions with each other: Who is speaking? Who is the audience? Who is the main character and how does he or she interact with the others in the situation? Question 8 allows you to add anything you find interesting.

AMY LAUGHS:

Imagine your perspective of the story of Cinderella is the setting of the *The Little Mermaid*. Your view would be incorrect. They were both royal settings, and both had a princess and a bad guy. However, one was underwater, brushing her hair with forks and blowing bubbles with a Jamaican crab while one was in a house, scrubbing the floor, and singing to clothed mice. When Ariel said she wanted to be where the people were, knowing she was an underwater mermaid sheds light on this story. You can see how the setting, plot, and characters play a huge role in understanding the meaning.

Question 9 asks you to identify God's role (presence) or His character shown in the story or set of verses. When reading any story, look for God's role. In some stories, this could be obvious. In other stories, such as the story of Rachel and Jacob, it might be harder to discover that God's role was an invisible presence to make Jacob humble and patient. Each story in the Bible teaches us something new about the character of God. The story of Noah's Ark teaches us about God's provision. The story of Job teaches us about God's restoration. The story of Paul teaches us about God's transforming power.

Question 10 asks you to summarize the story. Just record the details and facts like a detective would report them. You'll make the application to your life later.

The Peruse section of Step "4" will look like what you see on the next two pages. The words in italics represent the words you might write if you were doing the study.

4. FOLLOW THE Ps: PERUSE, PERSONALIZE, PURSUE

Peruse: Examine the details

Read the Scripture. Say it out loud. Ask God, *What do I need to know to be in this moment?*

1. Where is this taking place?
Nazareth (Luke 1:26)

2. How does the setting bring clarity to the meaning of the verse?
The Messiah would be rejected in His hometown. Jesus as the Messiah was rejected in Nazareth (Luke 4:24).

3. What is happening?
Gabriel, an angel, is telling Mary she will have a baby and that Elizabeth her cousin is having a baby.

4. Does the culture of that day play a role in understanding this passage? If so, how?
Yes! In Jesus' day, if a woman never had children, people believed that she was cursed of God. Elizabeth's pain of wanting children and not having any was coupled with the pain of serving God while everyone believed that she was cursed of God.
Mary couldn't believe she would have a baby as a virgin. Gabriel basically said: "God can do anything. Don't believe me? Even your too-old-to-even-think-of-having-a-baby cousin is pregnant too." If I looked at this verse and did not read the whole story, I would think: "With God by my side, nothing is impossible." But, that is not the culture, setting, context, or message God wants me to get. God took two situations that medicine, doctors, time, and methods could not remedy. He took a barren woman and a virgin and created life in each. Nothing is impossible with God. God took two impossible situations (a barren woman and a woman who'd never had sex) and created life in each. God turns the impossible into the possible. The culture and the overall story help me realize the impossibility of a virgin and barren woman having kids.

5. Who is speaking?
Gabriel, an angel.

6. Who is the audience?
Mary, Jesus' mother.

7. Who are the main characters, and how do they interact with others?
Mary. She is troubled and doubts the message Gabriel gave her. Elizabeth, Mary's cousin.

8. List any other interesting facts.
Gabriel was a powerful messenger from God. He was not a cuddly cherub.

9. What is God's role, or how is His character shown in this story?
He is the almighty and powerful God with whom nothing is impossible.

10. Summarize this Scripture passage.
Mary received some shocking news. She would be pregnant without being physically intimate with a man. She must have been shocked to see a real angel. But, God gave her a friend to help her through it all—her cousin, Elizabeth. Mary and John, Elizabeth's husband, had seen the angel and were experiencing things that others would find impossible.

PERSONALIZE: APPLY THE SPECIFICS

This second "P" will give you the opportunity to reflect on all the information you have collected and let the Holy Spirit show you how to apply this truth to your life. Personalizing the Scripture calls for a time of meditation as you apply the specific details Christ showed you. This will lead to repentance and commitment. You will be challenged to recall a time when you did not meet the standard God gave you in His Word.

You will have the opportunity to write a prayer of confession. You can take this time to remove the negative in your life and replace it with the positive. Take this time to remove thoughts or viewpoints that link God with impossibility. This includes limiting God to not provide admission to the college of your choice, not trusting God to provide a godly man for you, or not relying on God to be your Lord above everything else in your life that competes for first place. Replace lack of belief that God can do all things with hope as you confess and remove disbelief and doubt.

When our sample verse became personal to us, we realized that nothing was impossible with God. The areas that God showed Amy she had believed were impossible were different from the areas Mona believed were impossible. We both had to remove impossibility and replace it with the limitless possibilities of an active God, or we probably would have traded each other's doubts and fears.

Writing down your prayers and newfound truth helps the principles begin to gel within your mind and heart. Remember these pages are personal, so feel free to write all that is on your heart. You do not have to share them with anyone—not your group or even the person you meet with each week. You will celebrate when you look back at the pages later. There will be a sense of victory as you remember the miracle of God's Word revealed personally to you in the past and the difference it has made in the present.

MONA SHARES:

I love to reflect and write my prayers. I have a book in which I journal to Jesus about my day or things He teaches me. This book is bound, because I never want to tear out any pages in shame. I have a God whose mercies are new every morning (Lam. 3:22-23). He has thrown my sin as far as the East is from the West (Ps. 103:12). I can run to Him no matter what. You are in the same safe place when you confess your shortcomings, sin, or sorrow. Enjoy this section; God wants you to feel complete freedom in Him.

The Personalize section of Step "4" will look like what you see below and on the following pages. Remember, the italics represent what you might write.

PERSONALIZE: APPLY THE SPECIFICS

Consider how Jesus would have you apply this Scripture to your life.
Holy Spirit, please guide me into all truth as I'm considering what the angel told Mary. My wrist has been swollen for weeks. I love to write, cook, and do things up at the church. The enemy is telling me that I will always have this pain, but I choose to believe that if You could come to Earth and be born to a virgin, You can fix my wrist in Your perfect timing. Please increase my faith and my trust in You, my wonderfully active God.

Think of a time in the past when your life did not reflect this Scripture.
Dear Lord, the transition after graduation was tough. After several interviews and a failing economy, I'd decided to forget the dream job and was considering applying at Starbucks. Then, I chose to cling to this Scripture. I walked through a valley, but You—my active and wonderful Savior—have given me my dream job.

Confess your lack of following His Word and commit to follow Christ with the truth He has shown you.
Jesus, I thank you for loving me and my wrist. I am fearfully and wonderfully made. I choose to trust that You formed me in my mother's womb and know every cell in my body (Psalm 139). I will say Psalm 139 every time my wrist

hurts. I will remember that You are my loving Creator and thank You that my other wrist is not the size of a tomato. You alone are wise. I thank You that You are all-powerful and that truly nothing is impossible with You.

PURSUE: DELIGHT IN GOD

This whole time you have been examining details and applying specifics, but the point of reading the Bible is to meet a Person. You have missed the purpose of reading the Bible if you do not meet God, the One who is revealed in its pages. He longs for a friendship with you; not the kind of friendship where you know each other's names, but the kind of friendship where you recognize His voice and walk closely with Him. Christianity is not a list of do's and don'ts like DO go to church with your family. DON'T sleep with your boyfriend. DO be kind to others. DON'T wear two-piece bathing suits on church trips. DO pour into the lives of younger women.

These things may be important. But if you miss the fact that the God who died to save you wants to delight in you, then you have missed the most important thing. To delight in someone is to take pleasure in him or her. Do you see God this way? Do you picture God delighting in your thoughts, goals, and decisions? Do you take pleasure in His Words, commands, and character? The priceless part of this journey is that the God who made you and saved you loves you and delights in you. Through His Spirit and Word you can know Him and delight in Him in return. He made Himself known to you because He wants to be known! Your relationship with Him matters to Him.

Praise flows naturally when we know that the God of the universe placed all we need in the Bible. Thank Christ for His goodness; He did not leave you in the muck. He allowed you to learn from Him and know Him. Go ahead . . . express yourself with the excitement of a person who just exchanged the regret and guilt of limiting God with the confidence and acceptance that comes with trusting Him. Peace and joy come when we see the Scripture come alive in our lives. Worship is our response when we enter into an intimate conversation with the Lord. He speaks to us through His Word, and we respond with worship. In this section, you will write a prayer of response to God.

AMY SHARES:
I love to worship. Some of my most intimate times with God take place when I am sitting before Him quietly in worship and awe or singing at the top of my lungs in worship and delight. I love this part of the study. After God has shown me something specific from His Word, I want to celebrate.

Confidence in God's Word as the ultimate authority causes us to trust in the faithfulness of Christ and the reliability of His Word. Plus, realizing that God's Word can be understood when read gives us confidence knowing we can find an answer to any issue we face.

We've put together all the examples we've shown you over the last several chapters so you can see what a completed Discovery page looks like. Check it out on the following page.

DISCOVERY, DAY 2

TOPIC 1
IMPOSSIBLE

TOPIC 2
POSSIBLE

1. FOCUS ON THREE SCRIPTURES.

Using a concordance, look up several Scriptures that contain topic 1. Choose three verses that seem most interesting and applicable to you. Focus on those Scriptures, writing them word-for-word in the space provided below. Choose one to study by asking the Holy Spirit to show you which verse to study today. Circle or underline it.

Judges 6:5 (NIV)— "They came up with their livestock and their tents like swarms of locusts. It was impossible to count the men and their camels; they invaded the land to ravage it."

Luke 1:37— "For nothing will be impossible with God."

Hebrews 11:6— "And without faith it is impossible to please God, because anyone who comes to him must believe that he exists and that he rewards those who earnestly seek him."

2. FIND THE DEFINITION.

Find and write down the Hebrew or Greek definition for topic 1.

Luke 1:37- "Impossible"- Verb meaning void of power. (Found on Vine's page 321)

3. FILL IN THE SCRIPTURE.

Write your chosen Scripture again and replace the word or topic with the definition you found to amplify its meaning.

Luke 1:37— For nothing is impossible (void of power) with God.

4. FOLLOW THE Ps: PERUSE, PERSONALIZE, PURSUE

Peruse: Examine the Details

Read the Scripture. Say it out loud. Ask God, *What do I need to know to be in this moment?*

◼ LET'S GO!

1. Where is this taking place?
Nazareth (Luke 1:26)

2. How does the setting bring clarity to the meaning of the verse?
The Messiah would be rejected in His hometown. Jesus as the Messiah was rejected in Nazareth (Luke 4:24).

3. What is happening?
Gabriel, an angel, is telling Mary she will have a baby and that Elizabeth her cousin is having a baby.

4. Does the culture of that day play a role in understanding this passage? If so, how?
Yes! In Jesus' day, if a woman never had children, people believed that she was cursed of God. Elizabeth's pain of wanting children and not having any was coupled with the pain of serving God while everyone believed that she was cursed of God.
Mary couldn't believe she would have a baby as a virgin. Gabriel basically said: "God can do anything. Don't believe me? Even your too-old-to-even-think-of-having-a-baby cousin is pregnant too." If I looked at this verse and did not read the whole story, I would think: "With God by my side, nothing is impossible." But, that is not the culture, setting, context, or message God wants me to get. God took two situations that medicine, doctors, time, and methods could not remedy. He took a barren woman and a virgin and created life in each. Nothing is impossible with God. God took two impossible situations (a barren woman and a woman who'd never had sex) and created life in each. God turns the impossible into possible. The culture and the overall story help me realize the impossibility of a virgin and barren woman having kids.

5. Who is speaking?
Gabriel, an angel.

6. Who is the audience?
Mary, Jesus' mother.

7. Who are the main characters, and how do they interact with others?
Mary. She is troubled and doubts the message Gabriel gave her. Elizabeth, Mary's cousin.

8. List any other interesting facts.
Gabriel was a powerful messenger from God. He was not a cuddly cherub.

9. What is God's role, or how is His character shown in this story?
He is the almighty and powerful God with whom nothing is impossible.

10. Summarize this Scripture passage.
Mary received some shocking news. She would be pregnant without being physically intimate with a man. She must have been shocked to see a real angel. But, God gave her a friend to help her through it all—her cousin, Elizabeth. Mary and John, Elizabeth's husband, had seen the angel and were experiencing things that others would find impossible.

Personalize: Apply the specifics
• Consider how Jesus would have you apply this Scripture to your life.
Holy Spirit, please guide me into all truth as I'm considering what the angel told Mary. My wrist has been swollen for weeks. I love to write, cook, and do things up at the church. The enemy is telling me that I will always have this pain, but I choose to believe that if You could come to Earth and be born to a virgin, You can fix my wrist in Your perfect timing. Please increase my faith and my trust in You, my wonderfully active God.

• Think of a time in the past when your life did not reflect this Scripture.
Dear Lord, the transition after graduation was tough. After several interviews and a failing economy, I'd decided to forget the dream job and was considering applying at Starbucks. Then, I chose to cling to this Scripture. I walked through a valley, but You—my active and wonderful Savior—have given me my dream job.

• Confess your lack of following His Word and commit to follow Christ with the truth He has shown you.
Jesus, I thank you for loving me and my wrist. I am fearfully and wonderfully made. I choose to trust that You formed me in my mother's womb and know every cell in my body (Psalm 139). I will say Psalm 139 every time my wrist hurts. I will remember that You are my loving Creator and thank You that my other wrist is not the size of a tomato. You alone are wise. I thank You that You are all-powerful and that truly nothing is impossible with You.

Pursue: Delight in God
True worship comes from knowing that the God of the universe placed all we need to know in the Bible because He wanted to communicate

with us. He not only gave us the Bible, but He also gave us the Holy Spirit in our lives to make the Bible make sense and apply to our lives. We choose to delight in our good God. Write your words of worship to Him below.

Dear God, with a big fat wrist or a normal wrist, I know that You have plans to prosper me and not to harm me. I thank You for reminding me that you are in control. Even when my life feels out of control, I praise You that You are sovereign. Because You created life in a barren woman and in a virgin, I can stand on the promise that all things are possible with You. I choose to rest in You and trust my health and future to You. I LOVE YOU!

chapter seven

summary and sister day

WARNINGS FOR BIG SIS:
No gossip, even in the form of a prayer request. (For example, "Hey Molly, can we pray for Angelique? Yesterday, I heard she...")

Make sure you keep healthy boundaries. (If you're hearing "Honey, your lil sis has eaten dinner with us every night for two years straight," you may have a problem.)

WARNINGS FOR LIL SIS:
Transparency is great, but be sure not to share something personal about a family member without his or her permission. (It is NOT relevant to your discussion that your brother wore a superhero cape for five years.)

For four days the Holy Spirit has been teaching you and your sis separately. You will be so ready to talk to your sister and share all that you have learned. We will walk you through what a sister day will look like, but before we do, we wanted to clarify your roles a bit. This book is different from most others in that one female is not the main teacher and the other is not just listening. The mentoring is not "Sit still while I instill," but rather, "Let's sit together and mutually mentor each other."

BIG SIS ROLE:

You are not the teacher. Continually show the gal you meet with that the Holy Spirit is her teacher, guiding her into all truth as she reads God's Word and considers how He is speaking to her uniquely.

You are not a counselor. Your priority is to direct her to find God in His Word. Applaud her when she shares something that she learned (yes, clapping loudly is appropriate). Refrain from giving her the answers. Your words are beneficial, but the truth will set her free.

You are not her only friend. Small talk about her day is good, but the bulk of your time together should be centered around what both of you read and learned. Guide the conversation away from small talk or gossip by using phrases like, "Let's talk about that later," or "What's next?," or "I don't know the answer to that; let's both look for the answer over the coming week."

LIL SIS ROLE:

You do not have a lesser role. First Timothy 4:12 says: "No one should despise your youth; instead, you should be an example to the believers in speech, in conduct, in love, in faith, in purity. " You have the same Holy Spirit alive and working in and through you. Even though you will be studying the same topics, God will direct you to different Scriptures and teach you each something that is relevant for your life. Your big sis will be sharpened and encouraged by what you've learned.

You are not a counselor. We all have struggles no matter how old we are. Be a friend to your sis. Pray for her and love her, but remind her that God will heal our hearts and help our situations. Tell her that He's longing to give her the peace and answers she needs. Use sentences like, "I can't imagine going through that; let's see if God can show us something to help," or "I read something this week that helped me so much. Can I share it with you?" Remember, the same truth that sets you free will set her free too.

You are not lazy. Your role is not to sit back and listen to what she learned. Your consistent discipline in spending time in the Discovery

Pages will motivate your big sis to be all she can be, too. Listening to your excitement will give her hope in the future of our faith.

SISTER TIME!

On this day you will mentor and be mentored. The three actions in this day include: Pursue, Pray, and Perform.

Pursue

During the week, highlight different verses or definitions that you want to share with your sister. Many times you will not write down a single verse in common for the same topic, so be ready to talk and encourage each other with what the Lord has shown you. Discuss the personal applications and unique answers that God showed you during the week. Make sure to place all your weekly findings on Day 5 so you're prepared to let the sharpening begin.

Pray

Many people feel intimidated by praying out loud. We have included a list to pray through in this section if you need help getting started. Also use this time to pray for any personal needs. Your sis will love to lift you up in prayer. The personal connection happens here.

Perform

Each week offers an activity suggestion to give you an opportunity to serve each other. The weeks alternate: the big sis serves the first week, the lil sis takes the next week, and so on. We have provided some simple activities, but you can get creative and make up your own. The key here is not performance, but to show your sis a heart of service and that you were thinking about her and praying for her.

Another key part to the "Perform" section is accountability in memorizing Scripture together. Memorizing together allows for accountability and encouragement. Plus, God will show you something different about the verse each day as you meditate on different words or sections to memorize. Our words of wisdom can sometimes lack, but God's Word will never return void or empty.

Mutual mentoring is the key to leaving a legacy.

Sometimes you will need to agree to disagree. You and the woman you meet with may not always come to the same conclusion about a Scripture passage or topic. That's OK, as long as both viewpoints line up with Scripture. Bring to your meeting:
• Bible
• this book
• your weekly findings recorded on Day 5 of the Discovery Pages.

AMY RECALLS:

One of my "little sisters" and I have arranged to share our memorized verse for the week on Thursdays. One day she called me while she was waiting for the school bus. I was so thankful I had memorized my Scripture because I have a lil sis who is looking up to me and relying on me to hold her accountable to help her hide God's Word in her heart.

The Day 5 pages will look like this:

TOPIC 1	TOPIC 2
IMPOSSIBLE	**POSSIBLE**

Each sis should read one of these quotes out loud.

"I have found that there are three stages in every great work of God; first, it is impossible, then it is difficult, then it is done." —J. Hudson Taylor

"Faith sees the invisible, believes the unbelievable, and receives the impossible." —Corrie ten Boom

PURSUE!

My favorite verse this week:

Make sure you fill these in before you meet. The majority of your conversation will be spent answering these questions. Remember, if you begin to chase a rabbit, look at the questions on this page to guide you back. Also, you will share a lot when quoting your Scripture to each other. God speaks very clearly when you meditate on His Word.

The definition that surprised me the most:

My favorite thing I learned:

What God showed me about His character:

What verse I memorized and meditated on:

PRAY!

• Confess your disbelief that God will do impossible things for you.
• Ask God to increase your faith that everything is possible for Him.
• Praise God that He is powerful.
• Thank God that He is faithful to turn the impossible into possible.
• Ask God to do the impossible in a problem you are having today.

PERFORM!

(Big Sis . . . it's your turn)

Meet your sis at her favorite café or coffee shop. Remember to pick a quiet spot so you are not distracted by screaming babies or honking cars. Here are some suggestions for activities to highlight impossible and possible as you meet together:

Easy Breezy: Bring an apple. Cut the apple in half and look at the seeds. Say: It is impossible to think that one of these small seeds could create a tree. But in the hands of God, even a small seed can become not only a tree but an orchard!

Digging Deeper: Do the above analogy. Then, surprise your sis with a yummy apple dessert, such as apple pie or apple-cinnamon muffins. Put a cute tag on it that has Luke 1:37 and "We can make apple pies, but only God can make an orchard" written on it.

To help her memorize her verse for the next week, write "Verse for your Purse" at the top of five cute sticky notes. Instruct her to put one in her purse and every time she puts her purse down to read the verse once. She can place the rest of the notes in spots she will see often, such as her locker, mirror, computer monitor, and (let's be honest) the refrigerator. Each time she sees it, she should read her verse once and pray for help for you both to memorize the verse. Make five sticky notes for yourself too.

You can choose to do either the "Easy Breezy" or "Digging Deeper" activity.

LET THE DISCOVERY BEGIN!

For the next six weeks, we have chosen the topics for you. We have bolded each day's topic of study at the top of each Discovery Page; the last thing we would want is for someone to study the Greek meaning of death for a whole week!

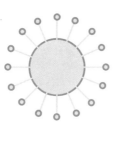
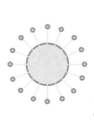

death vs. life

LESSON ONE

LESSON 1: DEATH VS. LIFE

Last year at junior high camp, our speaker spent an entire session reading verses that showed that sin always leads to death. He would read a verse and then say, "See, sin always leads to death." It was very powerful, and I was looking forward to getting back in the cabin with my eighth grade girls to ask questions and chat about all we'd heard. I will never forget sweet Maddie saying honestly: "I get that sin leads to death, but I worry and sometimes lie. And I'm still alive."

If you have confessed that Jesus is Lord and committed to serve and follow Him with your actions and life, then you are forgiven. The Bible says you have a new life in Christ. Second Corinthians 5:17 tells us that we are new creations.

So, can a live person be dead? Can someone who has been raised to life in Christ still sin and die?

There are different kinds of death—emotional death, spiritual death, and physical death. If you are reading this, then you aren't physically dead. If you are a follower of Christ and not simply a church attendee, then place your head on your pillow tonight with confidence—you aren't spiritually dead. But if you continually fear failure, battle unlimited insecurities, or whine and complain, you face emotional death. Consider the following two stories.

Typical day in the life of Sally:

Her eyes open. It's 7 a.m. Oh no! Are you kidding me?, she thinks. I set my alarm for 6. I overslept and can't read my Bible. God for sure will make me fail my test today. She looks in the mirror. Oh, another zit. For real? Why don't any of my friends have breakouts like me? All the boys want to sit by them, and the teachers always call on them because they are prettier. They even get all the solos in church choir because their parents are rich and can probably afford better soap or something.

In comes her mom who says, "Hi honey, ready to go?"

"Mom," Sally says, "I'm sick of you always rushing me and making me feel like I have to be perfect all the time." Of all the people who deserve to be popular and appreciated, it is me, but no, I'm stuck with a poor family. I'll never get a boyfriend, never get married, and never get a job other than babysitting because only pretty girls get those things.

Do you think Sally's story is exaggerated? Then you probably haven't taken the time to verbalize what you are thinking, or you haven't been listening closely to those around you. Matthew 12:34 says, "For the mouth speaks from the overflow of the heart." What you think, you will speak, and what you speak, you will probably act on. Sally is experiencing emotional death.

Typical day in the life of Suzy:

Her eyes open at 7 a.m. Oh no, I set my alarm for 6! I'll have to put on my make-up in the car while Mom drives me to school so I can have at least 10 minutes to read my Bible. I will do that instead of looking over my test again. I studied well, and I know God will honor my effort. She looks in the mirror. Oh, another zit. For real? I feel sooooo not cute right now. Wait. I will not have a bad day because of one zit. Where is my concealer? If I just swoop my bangs down a little more . . . wait . . . there . . . got it covered. If I don't point it out, no one will even notice.

In comes her mom. "Hi honey, ready to go?"

"Ready as ever," Suzy replies. "Can you please tell me how I can get rid of this zit? How did you deal with pimples when you were my age?" My mom always makes me feel better when I just talk to her.

Suzy's peace and calm in her situation shows us emotional maturity. Maybe you are reading this, and you haven't had a blemish in 30 years. But have you had a morning when you discovered a new gray hair or wrinkle? As women who are bombarded with media images of flawless women at every turn, we need to take advantage of the life we have in Christ. John 10:10 says, "I have come that they may have life and have it in abundance." Is your life abundant, or are your heart (emotions) and mind (thoughts) filled with death? As you read and reflect on the Scriptures each day this week, ask God to show you how you can think and speak differently to experience the life He died to give us. Whether you are looking at physical, spiritual, or emotional death, continually ask God to renew your mind so you can experience His peace.

> ## DISCOVERY, DAY 1
> | TOPIC 1 | TOPIC 2 |
> |---|---|
> | **DEATH** | **LIFE** |

1. FOCUS ON THREE SCRIPTURES.
Using a concordance, look up several Scriptures that contain topic 1. Choose three verses that seem most interesting and applicable to you. Focus on those Scriptures, writing them word-for-word in the space provided below. Choose one to study by asking the Holy Spirit to show you which verse to study today. Circle or underline it.

John 5:24 - Death
John 17:3 - Life

2. FIND THE DEFINITION.
Find and write down the English definition for topic 1.

3. FILL IN THE SCRIPTURE.
Write your chosen Scripture again and replace the word or topic with the definition you found to amplify its meaning.

4. FOLLOW THE Ps: PERUSE, PERSONALIZE, PURSUE
Peruse: Examine the details
Read the Scripture. Say it out loud. Ask God, *What do I need to know to be in this moment?*

1. Where is this taking place?

2. How does the setting bring clarity to the meaning of the verse?

3. What is happening?

4. Does the culture of that day play a role in understanding this passage? If so, how?

5. Who is speaking?

----

6. Who is the audience?

----

7. Who are the main characters, and how do they interact with others?

----

8. List any other interesting facts.

----

9. What is God's role, or how is His character shown in this story?

----

10. Summarize this Scripture passage.

Personalize: Apply the specifics
Consider how Jesus would have you apply this Scripture to your life.

Think of a time in the past when your life did not reflect this Scripture.

Confess your lack of following His Word in the past and commit to follow Christ with the truth He has shown you.

Pursue: Delight in God
True worship comes from knowing that the God of the universe placed all we need to know in the Bible because He wanted to communicate with us. He not only gave us the Bible, but He also gave us the Holy Spirit to make the Bible make sense and apply to our lives. We choose to delight in our good God. Write your words of worship to Him below.

DISCOVERY, DAY 2

TOPIC 1	TOPIC 2
DEATH	**LIFE**

1. FOCUS ON THREE SCRIPTURES.

Using a concordance, look up several Scriptures that contain topic 1. Choose three verses that seem most interesting and applicable to you. Focus on those Scriptures, writing them word-for-word in the space provided below. Choose one to study by asking the Holy Spirit to show you which verse to study today. Circle or underline it.

2. FIND THE DEFINITION.

Find and write down the Hebrew or Greek definition for topic 1.

3. FILL IN THE SCRIPTURE.

Write your chosen Scripture again and replace the word or topic with the definition you found to amplify its meaning.

4. FOLLOW THE Ps: PERUSE, PERSONALIZE, PURSUE

Peruse: Examine the details
Read the Scripture. Say it out loud. Ask God, *What do I need to know to be in this moment?*

1. Where is this taking place?

2. How does the setting bring clarity to the meaning of the verse?

3. What is happening?

4. Does the culture of that day play a role in understanding this passage? If so, how?

5. Who is speaking?

----

6. Who is the audience?

----

7. Who are the main characters, and how do they interact with others?

----

8. List any other interesting facts.

----

9. What is God's role, or how is His character shown in this story?

----

10. Summarize this Scripture passage.

Personalize: Apply the specifics

Consider how Jesus would have you apply this Scripture to your life.

Think of a time in the past when your life did not reflect this Scripture.

Confess your lack of following His Word in the past and commit to follow Christ with the truth He has shown you.

Pursue: Delight in God

True worship comes from knowing that the God of the universe placed all we need to know in the Bible because He wanted to communicate with us. He not only gave us the Bible, but He also gave us the Holy Spirit to make the Bible make sense and apply to our lives. We choose to delight in our good God. Write your words of worship to Him below.

> ### DISCOVERY, DAY 3
>
> TOPIC 1   TOPIC 2
> **DEATH**   **LIFE**

1. FOCUS ON THREE SCRIPTURES.

Using a concordance, look up several Scriptures that contain topic 2.
Choose three verses that seem most interesting and applicable to you.
Focus on those Scriptures, writing them word-for-word in the space
provided below. Choose one to study by asking the Holy Spirit to show
you which verse to study today. Circle or underline it.

2. FIND THE DEFINITION.

Find and write down the English definition for topic 2.

3. FILL IN THE SCRIPTURE.

Write your chosen Scripture again and replace the word or topic with the
definition you found to amplify its meaning.

4. FOLLOW THE Ps: PERUSE, PERSONALIZE, PURSUE

Peruse: Examine the details
Read the Scripture. Say it out loud. Ask God, *What do I need to know to be
in this moment?*

1. Where is this taking place?

2. How does the setting bring clarity to the meaning of the verse?

3. What is happening?

4. Does the culture of that day play a role in understanding this passage?
If so, how?

5. Who is speaking?

----

6. Who is the audience?

----

7. Who are the main characters, and how do they interact with others?

----

8. List any other interesting facts.

----

9. What is God's role, or how is His character shown in this story?

----

10. Summarize this Scripture passage.

Personalize: Apply the specifics
Consider how Jesus would have you apply this Scripture to your life.

Think of a time in the past when your life did not reflect this Scripture.

Confess your lack of following His Word in the past and commit to follow Christ with the truth He has shown you.

Pursue: Delight in God
True worship comes from knowing that the God of the universe placed all we need to know in the Bible because He wanted to communicate with us. He not only gave us the Bible, but He also gave us the Holy Spirit to make the Bible make sense and apply to our lives. We choose to delight in our good God. Write your words of worship to Him below.

DISCOVERY, DAY 4

TOPIC 1   TOPIC 2
DEATH   **LIFE**

1. FOCUS ON THREE SCRIPTURES.

Using a concordance, look up several Scriptures that contain topic 2.
Choose three verses that seem most interesting and applicable to you.
Focus on those Scriptures, writing them word-for-word in the space
provided below. Choose one to study by asking the Holy Spirit to show
you which verse to study today. Circle or underline it.

2. FIND THE DEFINITION.

Find and write down the Hebrew or Greek definition for topic 2.

3. FILL IN THE SCRIPTURE.

Write your chosen Scripture again and replace the word or topic with the
definition you found to amplify its meaning.

4. FOLLOW THE Ps: PERUSE, PERSONALIZE, PURSUE

Peruse: Examine the details
Read the Scripture. Say it out loud. Ask God, *What do I need to know to be
in this moment?*

1. Where is this taking place?

2. How does the setting bring clarity to the meaning of the verse?

3. What is happening?

4. Does the culture of that day play a role in understanding this passage?
If so, how?

5. Who is speaking?

6. Who is the audience?

7. Who are the main characters, and how do they interact with others?

8. List any other interesting facts.

9. What is God's role, or how is His character shown in this story?

10. Summarize this Scripture passage.

Personalize: Apply the specifics
Consider how Jesus would have you apply this Scripture to your life.

Think of a time in the past when your life did not reflect this Scripture.

Confess your lack of following His Word in the past and commit to follow Christ with the truth He has shown you.

Pursue: Delight in God
True worship comes from knowing that the God of the universe placed all we need to know in the Bible because He wanted to communicate with us. He not only gave us the Bible, but He also gave us the Holy Spirit to make the Bible make sense and apply to our lives. We choose to delight in our good God. Write your words of worship to Him below.

DISCOVERY, DAY 5

TOPIC 1	TOPIC 2
DEATH	**LIFE**

"We are acceptable with God not because we have obeyed, or because we have promised to give up things, but because of the death of Jesus and in no other way." —Oswald Chambers[1]

"The whole church of God gains when the members that compose it begin to seek a better and higher life." —A.W. Tozer[2]

Each sis should read one of these quotes out loud.

PURSUE!

My favorite verse this week:

The definition that surprised me the most:

My favorite thing I learned:

What God showed me about His character:

Make sure you fill these in before you meet. The majority of your conversation will be spent answering these questions. If you become distracted, look at the questions on this page to guide you back. Also, you will share a lot when quoting your Scripture to each other. God speaks clearly when you meditate on His Word.

PRAY!

Read 1 John 5:11-13.
• Confess any thoughts or words you have that are death more than life.
• Ask God to forgive you and help you to be filled with life instead of death.
• Praise God that He is life. Thank God that you have the opportunity to walk in life and not death.
• Ask God to show you ways that you can show others that He is alive and that you are also alive in Him today.

PERFORM!

(Big Sis, it's your turn)
Here are some suggestions for activities to highlight death or life as you meet together:

Easy Breezy: Gather one or two magazines to discuss which activities described or pictured will lead to emotional, physical, or spiritual death. (This should lead to GREAT discussion). Make sure you are pointing back to what you learned this week instead of letting this look like a rerun of a gossip show.

Digging Deeper: Give your sis a journal. Write verses that you learned and meditated on about the difference in death and life along the top of several different pages sprinkled throughout. Add a few words about what God showed you from each one. Encourage her to write her thoughts in it, and then have her check to see if they contain more death or life. To end, make a commitment to choose to live an abundant life. We cannot control our circumstances, but we can control the way we view them.

Our precious women's ministry director at church, Debbie Stuart, once said: "It is not your problem that is the problem, it is your perspective of the problem." Choose to believe Christ. Choose life so that you may live. Pray that God would cause you to call out to Him when a "death thought" enters your mind. Pray that then you would read His Word. Pray then that you would call your sis for encouragement.

1. Oswald Chambers, *My Utmost for His Highest*
2. A.W. Tozer, *The Pursuit of God*

"See, today I have set before you life and prosperity, death and adversity. For I am commanding you today to love the Lord your God, to walk in His ways, and to keep His commands, statutes, and ordinances, so that you may live and multiply, and the Lord your God may bless you in the land you are entering to possess . . . Choose life so that you and your descendants may live, love the Lord your God, obey Him, and remain faithful to Him. For He is your life, and He will prolong your life in the land the Lord swore to give to your fathers Abraham, Isaac, and Jacob."
—Deuteronomy 30:15-16,19b-20

fear vs. faith

LESSON TWO

LESSON 2: FEAR VS. FAITH

I was sitting and staring at my blank computer screen, thinking about you as you engage in *Table for Two*. As I considered how to proceed, my thoughts wandered to the wonderful impact this study tool could have on your life. Then a random negative thought came.

All of a sudden I realized I was not only writing about fear, I was now in fear. I knew I had to pray for Jesus to help me. You see, I spent many years captive to the unrelenting torment of fear. The enemy still tries to sneak it in (like as I was writing this), but I have a God who tells me over 360 times in His Word that I should not fear. Let me be clear: He never said that I wouldn't feel fear. He just wants me to be confident knowing I don't have to act on fear when it shows up. The best part is that He shows me how to fight it with faith.

The battlefield is in the mind. Fear and faith are very similar; they both expect something to happen in the future. However, their origins, purposes, and outcomes are on opposite sides of the battlefield.

Fear wants to control, oppress, and dominate. Suggestion is its first strike. Terrorism is an example of fear used as a weapon. Cheaply and quickly, it can strike the mind of anyone. Satan loves nothing more than to sneak up and suggest that you need to be afraid.

Fear has invaded our culture. Depression, suicide, the economy—gloomy statistics are all a part of everyday life. It is even considered loving to worry about your family.

How can we combat this disease of fear? Faith is the antidote. We fight fear with faith. Hebrews 11:1 reveals that faith is the opposite of fear. Fear controls; faith releases into the hands of a trustworthy God. Faith grows confidence, which builds more faith, making us stronger for the battle.

How do we get victory over what's poisoning our minds? Let's start eradicating fear with a few basic steps that will have us marching in faith with fearless confidence.

Now faith is the reality of what is hoped for, the proof of what is not seen.
—Hebrews 11:1

Write this on your bathroom mirror with a dry erase marker. For each day circle the word you will meditate on and ask God about it.

MAKE A CHOICE

God wants us to renew our minds by taking captive every thought that is not based in truth. To accomplish that, we must make a choice to think beyond what we see. Being a visual girl, I always picture trees as they cast shadows on the ground. Am I looking past the dark shadows (fear) to the light (faith)? I get to choose, and so do you.

FIND GOD'S FAITH WORD

The next time you find yourself gripped with fear, stop and find out what God's Word says about it. Our study this week will equip you to find Scriptures about faith.

BELIEVE AND SPEAK THE SCRIPTURES

God wrote the Bible for your protection, instruction, and wisdom. Do you know what fear fears? The authority of God's Word. Fear is quick to leave as you speak confident faith-filled truths. God has given His children the authority to use His Word just like Jesus did. During His 40 days in the desert, Jesus used only the Word of God to combat the Devil. We have the same ability. Fight fearful thoughts with words, the very words of God. The next time the Devil whispers thoughts of fear and doubt, speak the Word of God, and he will flee.

BE BRAVE

Step out in confident faith, believing God provides. The promises in the Bible are abundant and rich. Take time to find some that move you to faith. Then continue to hope in faith.

We also need to be brave as we step out in faith and believe God. In Beth Moore's outstanding book *Believing God,* she gives us faith-filled beliefs that still flow across my lips as weapons against Satan:

God is who He says He is.
God can do what He says He can do.
I am who God says I am.
I can do all things through Christ.
God's Word is alive and active in me. [1]

As I finish writing this introduction, fear is gone. I know what to do when I hear the sorry voice of the enemy tempting me. I stop, spend time in the Word, and speak what I believe in faith. This chapter is perfectly placed in this book. Studying these two topics will give your confidence a kick-start. Then when Satan tries to contaminate your pursuit of God, you will know what to do. Hit him with your best shot from the arsenal of God's Word. Fire away!

1. Beth Moore, *Believing God*, (Nashville, Tenn.: Broadman & Holman, 2004), p. 43.

> ## DISCOVERY, DAY 1
> | TOPIC 1 | TOPIC 2 |
> |---------|---------|
> | **FEAR** | **FAITH** |

1. FOCUS ON THREE SCRIPTURES.

Using a concordance, look up several Scriptures that contain topic 1. Choose three verses that seem most interesting and applicable to you. Focus on those Scriptures, writing them word-for-word in the space provided below. Choose one to study by asking the Holy Spirit to show you which verse to study today. Circle or underline it.

2. FIND THE DEFINITION.

Find and write down the English definition for topic 1.

3. FILL IN THE SCRIPTURE.

Write your chosen Scripture again and replace the word or topic with the definition you found to amplify its meaning.

4. FOLLOW THE Ps: PERUSE, PERSONALIZE, PURSUE

Peruse: Examine the details

Read the Scripture. Say it out loud. Ask God, *What do I need to know to be in this moment?*

1. Where is this taking place?

2. How does the setting bring clarity to the meaning of the verse?

3. What is happening?

4. Does the culture of that day play a role in understanding this passage? If so, how?

5. Who is speaking?

----

6. Who is the audience?

----

7. Who are the main characters, and how do they interact with others?

----

8. List any other interesting facts.

----

9. What is God's role, or how is His character shown in this story?

----

10. Summarize this Scripture passage.

Personalize: Apply the specifics
Consider how Jesus would have you apply this Scripture to your life.

Think of a time in the past when your life did not reflect this Scripture.

Confess your lack of following His Word in the past and commit to follow Christ with the truth He has shown you.

Pursue: Delight in God
True worship comes from knowing that the God of the universe placed all we need to know in the Bible because He wanted to communicate with us. He not only gave us the Bible, but He also gave us the Holy Spirit to make the Bible make sense and apply to our lives. We choose to delight in our good God. Write your words of worship to Him below.

DISCOVERY, DAY 2

TOPIC 1	TOPIC 2
FEAR	**FAITH**

1. FOCUS ON THREE SCRIPTURES.

Using a concordance, look up several Scriptures that contain topic 1. Choose three verses that seem most interesting and applicable to you. Focus on those Scriptures, writing them word-for-word in the space provided below. Choose one to study by asking the Holy Spirit to show you which verse to study today. Circle or underline it.

2. FIND THE DEFINITION.

Find and write down the Hebrew or Greek definition for topic 1.

3. FILL IN THE SCRIPTURE.

Write your chosen Scripture again and replace the word or topic with the definition you found to amplify its meaning.

4. FOLLOW THE Ps: PERUSE, PERSONALIZE, PURSUE

Peruse: Examine the details
Read the Scripture. Say it out loud. Ask God, *What do I need to know to be in this moment?*

1. Where is this taking place?

2. How does the setting bring clarity to the meaning of the verse?

3. What is happening?

4. Does the culture of that day play a role in understanding this passage? If so, how?

5. Who is speaking?

- -

6. Who is the audience?

- -

7. Who are the main characters, and how do they interact with others?

- -

- -

8. List any other interesting facts.

- -

- -

9. What is God's role, or how is His character shown in this story?

- -

10. Summarize this Scripture passage.

- -

- -

- -

- -

Personalize: Apply the specifics
Consider how Jesus would have you apply this Scripture to your life.

- -

- -

Think of a time in the past when your life did not reflect this Scripture.

- -

- -

Confess your lack of following His Word in the past and commit to follow Christ with the truth He has shown you.

- -

- -

Pursue: Delight in God
True worship comes from knowing that the God of the universe placed all we need to know in the Bible because He wanted to communicate with us. He not only gave us the Bible, but He also gave us the Holy Spirit to make the Bible make sense and apply to our lives. We choose to delight in our good God. Write your words of worship to Him below.

- -

- -

- -

- -

> ## DISCOVERY, DAY 3
> | TOPIC 1 | TOPIC 2 |
> |---------|---------|
> | **FEAR** | **FAITH** |

1. FOCUS ON THREE SCRIPTURES.
Using a concordance, look up several Scriptures that contain topic 2. Choose three verses that seem most interesting and applicable to you. Focus on those Scriptures, writing them word-for-word in the space provided below. Choose one to study by asking the Holy Spirit to show you which verse to study today. Circle or underline it.

2. FIND THE DEFINITION.
Find and write down the English definition for topic 2.

3. FILL IN THE SCRIPTURE.
Write your chosen Scripture again and replace the word or topic with the definition you found to amplify its meaning.

4. FOLLOW THE Ps: PERUSE, PERSONALIZE, PURSUE
Peruse: Examine the details
Read the Scripture. Say it out loud. Ask God, *What do I need to know to be in this moment?*

1. Where is this taking place?

2. How does the setting bring clarity to the meaning of the verse?

3. What is happening?

4. Does the culture of that day play a role in understanding this passage? If so, how?

5. Who is speaking?

----

6. Who is the audience?

----

7. Who are the main characters, and how do they interact with others?

----

8. List any other interesting facts.

----

9. What is God's role, or how is His character shown in this story?

----

10. Summarize this Scripture passage.

Personalize: Apply the specifics
Consider how Jesus would have you apply this Scripture to your life.

Think of a time in the past when your life did not reflect this Scripture.

Confess your lack of following His Word in the past and commit to follow Christ with the truth He has shown you.

Pursue: Delight in God
True worship comes from knowing that the God of the universe placed all we need to know in the Bible because He wanted to communicate with us. He not only gave us the Bible, but He also gave us the Holy Spirit to make the Bible make sense and apply to our lives. We choose to delight in our good God. Write your words of worship to Him below.

DISCOVERY, DAY 4

TOPIC 1	TOPIC 2
FEAR	**FAITH**

1. FOCUS ON THREE SCRIPTURES.

Using a concordance, look up several Scriptures that contain topic 2. Choose three verses that seem most interesting and applicable to you. Focus on those Scriptures, writing them word-for-word in the space provided below. Choose one to study by asking the Holy Spirit to show you which verse to study today. Circle or underline it.

2. FIND THE DEFINITION.

Find and write down the Hebrew or Greek definition for topic 2.

3. FILL IN THE SCRIPTURE.

Write your chosen Scripture again and replace the word or topic with the definition you found to amplify its meaning.

4. FOLLOW THE Ps: PERUSE, PERSONALIZE, PURSUE

Peruse: Examine the details

Read the Scripture. Say it out loud. Ask God, *What do I need to know to be in this moment?*

1. Where is this taking place?

2. How does the setting bring clarity to the meaning of the verse?

3. What is happening?

4. Does the culture of that day play a role in understanding this passage? If so, how?

5. Who is speaking?

- -

6. Who is the audience?

- -

7. Who are the main characters, and how do they interact with others?

- -

- -

8. List any other interesting facts.

- -

- -

9. What is God's role, or how is His character shown in this story?

- -

10. Summarize this Scripture passage.

- -

- -

- -

Personalize: Apply the specifics

Consider how Jesus would have you apply this Scripture to your life.

- -

Think of a time in the past when your life did not reflect this Scripture.

- -

- -

Confess your lack of following His Word in the past and commit to follow Christ with the truth He has shown you.

- -

- -

Pursue: Delight in God

True worship comes from knowing that the God of the universe placed all we need to know in the Bible because He wanted to communicate with us. He not only gave us the Bible, but He also gave us the Holy Spirit to make the Bible make sense and apply to our lives. We choose to delight in our good God. Write your words of worship to Him below.

- -

- -

- -

- -

DISCOVERY, DAY 5

TOPIC 1	TOPIC 2
FEAR	**FAITH**

"You make me want to be brave." —"Brave" by Nichole Nordeman

"Do not fear, for I am with you; do not be afraid, for I am your God."
—*Isaiah 41:10*

PURSUE!

My favorite verse this week:

- -

- -

The definition that surprised me the most:

- -

- -

My favorite thing I learned:

- -

- -

What God showed me about His character:

- -

- -

PRAY!

- Confess that fear has been too common in your life. Describe some of your fears.
- Ask God to arm you with all you need to live a peaceful and fearless life of faith.
- Praise God for loving you and for never leaving you unequipped or alone.
- Thank God for His precious Word, the Bible. What a glorious gift that it contains the very breath of the One who readily gives us the faith we need.

PERFORM!

(Lil Sis, it's your turn.)
Here are some suggestions for activities to highlight fear or faith as you meet together:

Easy Breezy:

Skip buying coffee when you meet this time. Spend the money on the purchase of index cards and a container for each of you. These are available very reasonably at office supply stores. After your discussion, write verses on the index card that you are going to memorize. (This should be done weekly.) These are your faith arsenal. You could even label your container or box, "Faith Arsenal." When one of you is struggling, call the other for a quick verse. Doing this throughout your study through *Table for Two* will keep you armed and ready for any faith challenge.

Digging Deeper:

Create a playlist of songs that produce faith for you and your sis. Songs like "Brave" by Nichole Nordeman will leave you and your sis singing words that will grow even more faith in both of you. Remember that faith comes by hearing and doing the Word of God. God's Word is powerful, even through song.

To end your time together, make a commitment to live a faith-filled (not fear-filled) life. Pray together. Pray that God would lead you to call out to Him when a fearful thought enters your mind. Pray that you would read His Word, then call your sis for encouragement when fearful thoughts assault you.

darkness vs. light

LESSON THREE

LESSON 3: DARKNESS VS. LIGHT

If you spent any time in church as a child, then at some point you probably learned the song "This Little Light of Mine." You held up your finger and said something about not letting Satan blow it out and that you would let your light shine. Even though I started singing that at such a young age, the concept of light and dark still affects me even as I grow older. Actually, there are few analogies that illustrate the definition of an opposite quite like light and dark.

Imagine you are walking into a room with no light—there are no windows, no light fixtures, no chances of illumination. For ten seconds, close your eyes and envision that you are walking around in this room with no light.

That was only for ten seconds. Below, write some descriptions of your thoughts of life without light, including adjectives, needs you couldn't meet, and everyday conveniences you just could not enjoy.

When I imagine a world without light, the first word I think of is *confusion*. You would constantly be stepping on, running into, or tripping over something. I also think of *frustration*. Cooking would be dangerous—you could burn your hand, chop off a finger, or accidentally substitute the wrong ingredients. Forget ever fixing your hair, looking in a mirror, or actually knowing what you look like.

I also think of *shame*. Most of the things that we are ashamed of have happened in dark places—sex, abuse, etc. I think of *depression*. People who are depressed feed their depression by sitting in a dark home. I think of *hate*—a dark heart. I think of evil in a hurtful world.

God knew that we would need the beauty of a sunset to give us a sense of awe at His creation. He knew that we would need to be able to see others to know when to reach out to them. God knows how to meet the needs of His people. That is why He said, "Let there be light."

Darkness and light are not only opposite in a physical way, but the Bible continually uses the opposites of dark and light to describe much bigger concepts. We know you will enjoy perusing the topics of darkness and light this week.

> ### DISOVERY, DAY 1
> | TOPIC 1 | TOPIC 2 |
> |---|---|
> | **DARKNESS** | **LIGHT** |

1. FOCUS ON THREE SCRIPTURES.

Using a concordance, look up several Scriptures that contain topic 1. Choose three verses that seem most interesting and applicable to you. Focus on those Scriptures, writing them word-for-word in the space provided below. Choose one to study by asking the Holy Spirit to show you which verse to study today. Circle or underline it.

2. FIND THE DEFINITION.

Find and write down the English definition for topic 1.

3. FILL IN THE SCRIPTURE.

Write your chosen Scripture again and replace the word or topic with the definition you found to amplify its meaning.

4. FOLLOW THE Ps: PERUSE, PERSONALIZE, PURSUE

Peruse: Examine the details
Read the Scripture. Say it out loud. Ask God, *What do I need to know to be in this moment?*

1. Where is this taking place?

2. How does the setting bring clarity to the meaning of the verse?

3. What is happening?

4. Does the culture of that day play a role in understanding this passage? If so, how?

5. Who is speaking?

----

6. Who is the audience?

----

7. Who are the main characters, and how do they interact with others?

----

8. List any other interesting facts.

----

9. What is God's role, or how is His character shown in this story?

----

10. Summarize this Scripture passage.

Personalize: Apply the specifics
Consider how Jesus would have you apply this Scripture to your life.

Think of a time in the past when your life did not reflect this Scripture.

Confess your lack of following His Word in the past and commit to follow
Christ with the truth He has shown you.

Pursue: Delight in God
True worship comes from knowing that the God of the universe placed
all we need to know in the Bible because He wanted to communicate
with us. He not only gave us the Bible, but He also gave us the Holy Spirit
to make the Bible make sense and apply to our lives. We choose to delight
in our good God. Write your words of worship to Him below.

DISCOVERY, DAY 2

TOPIC 1   TOPIC 2

DARKNESS   **LIGHT**

1. FOCUS ON THREE SCRIPTURES.

Using a concordance, look up several Scriptures that contain topic 1. Choose three verses that seem most interesting and applicable to you. Focus on those Scriptures, writing them word-for-word in the space provided below. Choose one to study by asking the Holy Spirit to show you which verse to study today. Circle or underline it.

2. FIND THE DEFINITION.

Find and write down the Hebrew or Greek definition for topic 1.

3. FILL IN THE SCRIPTURE.

Write your chosen Scripture again and replace the word or topic with the definition you found to amplify its meaning.

4. FOLLOW THE Ps: PERUSE, PERSONALIZE, PURSUE

Peruse: Examine the details

Read the Scripture. Say it out loud. Ask God, *What do I need to know to be in this moment?*

1. Where is this taking place?

2. How does the setting bring clarity to the meaning of the verse?

3. What is happening?

4. Does the culture of that day play a role in understanding this passage? If so, how?

5. Who is speaking?

----

6. Who is the audience?

----

7. Who are the main characters, and how do they interact with others?

----

8. List any other interesting facts.

----

9. What is God's role, or how is His character shown in this story?

----

10. Summarize this Scripture passage.

Personalize: Apply the specifics
Consider how Jesus would have you apply this Scripture to your life.

Think of a time in the past when your life did not reflect this Scripture.

Confess your lack of following His Word in the past and commit to follow Christ with the truth He has shown you.

Pursue: Delight in God
True worship comes from knowing that the God of the universe placed all we need to know in the Bible because He wanted to communicate with us. He not only gave us the Bible, but He also gave us the Holy Spirit to make the Bible make sense and apply to our lives. We choose to delight in our good God. Write your words of worship to Him below.

> ## DISCOVERY, DAY 3
>
> | TOPIC 1 | TOPIC 2 |
> | --- | --- |
> | **DARKNESS** | **LIGHT** |

1. FOCUS ON THREE SCRIPTURES.

Using a concordance, look up several Scriptures that contain topic 2.
Choose three verses that seem most interesting and applicable to you.
Focus on those Scriptures, writing them word-for-word in the space
provided below. Choose one to study by asking the Holy Spirit to show
you which verse to study today. Circle or underline it.

2. FIND THE DEFINITION.

Find and write down the English definition for topic 2.

3. FILL IN THE SCRIPTURE.

Write your chosen Scripture and replace the word or topic with the definition you found to amplify its meaning.

4. FOLLOW THE Ps: PERUSE, PERSONALIZE, PURSUE

Peruse: Examine the details
Read the Scripture. Say it out loud. Ask God, *What do I need to know to be
in this moment?*

1. Where is this taking place?

2. How does the setting bring clarity to the meaning of the verse?

3. What is happening?

4. Does the culture of that day play a role in understanding this passage?
If so, how?

5. Who is speaking?

----

6. Who is the audience?

----

7. Who are the main characters, and how do they interact with others?

----

8. List any other interesting facts.

----

9. What is God's role, or how is His character shown in this story?

----

10. Summarize this Scripture passage.

Personalize: Apply the specifics

Consider how Jesus would have you apply this Scripture to your life.

Think of a time in the past when your life did not reflect this Scripture.

Confess your lack of following His Word in the past and commit to follow Christ with the truth He has shown you.

Pursue: Delight in God

True worship comes from knowing that the God of the universe placed all we need to know in the Bible because He wanted to communicate with us. He not only gave us the Bible, but He also gave us the Holy Spirit to make the Bible make sense and apply to our lives. We choose to delight in our good God. Write your words of worship to Him below.

DISCOVERY, DAY 4

TOPIC 1	TOPIC 2
DARKNESS	**LIGHT**

1. FOCUS ON THREE SCRIPTURES.

Using a concordance, look up several Scriptures that contain topic 2. Choose three verses that seem most interesting and applicable to you. Focus on those Scriptures, writing them word-for-word in the space provided below. Choose one to study by asking the Holy Spirit to show you which verse to study today. Circle or underline it.

2. FIND THE DEFINITION.

Find and write down the Hebrew or Greek definition for topic 2.

- -

3. FILL IN THE SCRIPTURE.

Write your chosen Scripture again and replace the word or topic with the definition you found to amplify its meaning.

4. FOLLOW THE Ps: PERUSE, PERSONALIZE, PURSUE

Peruse: Examine the details
Read the Scripture. Say it out loud. Ask God, *What do I need to know to be in this moment?*

1. Where is this taking place?

- -

2. How does the setting bring clarity to the meaning of the verse?

- -

3. What is happening?

- -

4. Does the culture of that day play a role in understanding this passage? If so, how?

- -

- -

- -

5. Who is speaking?

----

6. Who is the audience?

----

7. Who are the main characters, and how do they interact with others?

----

8. List any other interesting facts.

----

9. What is God's role, or how is His character shown in this story?

----

10. Summarize this Scripture passage.

Personalize: Apply the specifics

Consider how Jesus would have you apply this Scripture to your life.

Think of a time in the past when your life did not reflect this Scripture.

Confess your lack of following His Word in the past and commit to follow Christ with the truth He has shown you.

Pursue: Delight in God

True worship comes from knowing that the God of the universe placed all we need to know in the Bible because He wanted to communicate with us. He not only gave us the Bible, but He also gave us the Holy Spirit to make the Bible make sense and apply to our lives. We choose to delight in our good God. Write your words of worship to Him below.

> ## DISOVERY, DAY 5
> ## DARKNESS VS. LIGHT

"A man can no more diminish God's glory by refusing to worship Him than a lunatic can put out the sun by scribbling 'darkness' on the walls of his cell."
—*C.S. Lewis*

"Into marvelous light I'm running!" —*"Marvelous Light" by Charlie Hall*

PURSUE!

My favorite verse this week:

The definition that surprised me the most:

My favorite thing I learned:

What God showed me about His character:

PRAY!

• Confess that you were in darkness before you knew God.
• Thank God that His light has taken you out of darkness and into His light.
• Ask God to show you ways that you can shine His light in a dark world today.

PERFORM!

(Big Sis, it's your turn.)
Here are some suggestions for activities to highlight darkness and light as you meet together:

Easy Breezy: Meet for lunch and bring a little votive candle for the table. Let your light shine as you share what you learned this week. This will be a great opportunity to share what you are doing with people who ask why you have a candle.

Digging Deeper: Prepare a candlelit dinner for your sis. This will give you an opportunity to serve her and to truly see how great the contrast of light and dark is! (Not a chef? Dessert and coffee are great.)

To end, make a commitment to choose to walk in light rather than in darkness. We cannot control the fact that we live in a dark world, but we can control whether we shine and stand out or diminish our light by joining in and following the crowd.

A friend shared a story about growing up as a missionary kid in Africa. Their "church" was a cement slab, four poles, and a thatched roof. One light bulb hung from the middle part of the roof. The single bulb gave light to the entire slab, but when someone stepped off of the cement, he needed a flashlight to see where to take his next step. Our friend said, "We sang and listened to preaching for hours. If you stood close to the end of the cement, you could see some people walk close as if they wanted to come in or at least listen to check out what we were doing. When someone joined us, they were renouncing the religion of their family and tribe. Some came in and accepted Christ. Some continued to walk in the dark."

Read 1 Thessalonians 5:5,9-10.

Complete this sentence from verse 5: You are all sons of _____ and sons of the _____. We're not of the _____ or of _____.

Remember who you are: a daughter of the one true Light. You have been delivered. You have been transferred to the Kingdom of light (Col. 1:13-14). Do not live in shame; the Father of lights is the lifter of your head. You cannot live in darkness because He has called you into His marvelous light. Choose to step out of the darkness into light and life. Choose books, songs, and movies that encourage you and remind you to walk in the light. Choose friends who challenge you to not look like a daughter of darkness. Pray that God would cause you to call out to Him when darkness seems more appealing than light. Pray that in those situations you would read His Word and call your sis for encouragement.

jealousy vs. contentment

LESSON FOUR

LESSON 4: JEALOUSY VS. CONTENTMENT

Hot summer days always drain Julie, but this one was taking away all she had. Plopping down on the sofa, she covered her eyes and fought back tears that were hotter than the Texas heat outside.

Another promotion lost, she thought to herself. *I know I am as good as that Kelly chick. But just because she's young and can wear tight skirts . . . ugh. And me with college tuition to pay. If they think I'm going to work with that girl on the new project, they've got another thing coming.*

The front door slams and Julie leans over to see her 20-something, beautiful daughter Chloe silently crying with her head slumped and hands over her face. Julie forgets her own troubles and calls out to her daughter, "Honey, what is the matter?" Chloe walks over and lifts her tear-stained hand to her mother, exposing the message on her phone.

Maddie: I have something to tell you

Chloe: I have a minute. What's up?

Maddie: The most wonderful thing happened today

Chloe: ???

Maddie: Max asked me to marry him today!

Maddie: Chloe are you there?

Chloe: Yes

Maddie: Can you meet for coffee? I want to tell you everything!

"I just can't go, Mom," she sobs. Julie knows why. Chloe has been a bridesmaid more than a few times. "I want to be happy for her," Chloe said, "but I am ashamed to say I am jealous. Mom, will I ever find a husband?"

Wow. These girls have had a hard day. The things they were expecting and wanting for themselves were happening to someone else. Jealousy was setting in quickly. They needed to change their thinking before jobs and relationships were lost. What they needed was a new attitude.

Where does a new attitude come from? A membership at the gym? Six years in counseling? Maybe a tongue lashing from grandma? Nope. It comes from God's love for us.

I know you're thinking: " Sounds good, but this green-eyed monster just keeps eating at me." I totally get it. Jealousy is one of the enemy's favorite weapons. It is so sneaky; he wants you to believe little lies that nibble at your trust in God like: "I can't believe she . . .," or "You're not smart enough/young enough/old enough to . . .," or "I don't deserve to get my dream because . . ."

The enemy wants you to agree with those negative thoughts. He wants you to believe that God either won't take care of you, can't take care of you, or, worst of all, doesn't want to take care of you. If you want to defeat jealousy, you're going to have to fight back. Your weapon for the fight is the Word of God. Change and renew your inner thoughts based on what God says, and you will achieve contentment.

When it comes to wonderful things or fulfilled desires, God doesn't have a closet in the sky that is limited to one of each thing. He doesn't run out of good things. Just because another friend gets something you really want, like a boyfriend or a good relationship with her parents, doesn't mean you'll never have it. What God does have is an amazing plan for you. Realizing this is a really important part of moving from jealousy into contentment.

On your sister day, you will look at Jeremiah 29:11. It is a popular verse because it dispels the lie that God won't, can't, or doesn't want to take care of you. Jealousy desires what everyone else has. It is like being in a rain shower and trying to catch the raindrops falling on someone else's head. Look up sister; your own drops are falling.

The bottom line is that God has an individual plan prepared only for you. Put your trust and confidence in that truth. As you work through jealousy and contentment this week, allow the Holy Spirit to rain down His truth and wash away any jealousy in you with His love. And if it just happens to rain at your house this week, go out and feel the rain on your skin.

DISCOVERY, DAY 1

TOPIC 1	TOPIC 2
JEALOUSY	**CONTENTMENT**

1. FOCUS ON THREE SCRIPTURES.

Using a concordance, look up several Scriptures that contain topic 1. Choose three verses that seem most interesting and applicable to you. Focus on those Scriptures, writing them word-for-word in the space provided below. Choose one to study by asking the Holy Spirit to show you which verse to study today. Circle or underline it.

2. FIND THE DEFINITION.

Find and write down the English definition for topic 1.

3. FILL IN THE SCRIPTURE.

Write your chosen Scripture again and replace the word or topic with the definition you found to amplify its meaning.

4. FOLLOW THE Ps: PERUSE, PERSONALIZE, PURSUE

Peruse: Examine the details
Read the Scripture. Say it out loud. Ask God, *What do I need to know to be in this moment?*

1. Where is this taking place?

2. How does the setting bring clarity to the meaning of the verse?

3. What is happening?

4. Does the culture of that day play a role in understanding this passage? If so, how?

5. Who is speaking?

----

6. Who is the audience?

----

7. Who are the main characters, and how do they interact with others?

----

8. List any other interesting facts.

----

9. What is God's role, or how is His character shown in this story?

----

10. Summarize this Scripture passage.

Personalize: Apply the specifics
Consider how Jesus would have you apply this Scripture to your life.

Think of a time in the past when your life did not reflect this Scripture.

Confess your lack of following His Word in the past and commit to follow Christ with the truth He has shown you.

Pursue: Delight in God
True worship comes from knowing that the God of the universe placed all we need to know in the Bible because He wanted to communicate with us. He not only gave us the Bible, but He also gave us the Holy Spirit to make the Bible make sense and apply to our lives. We choose to delight in our good God. Write your words of worship to Him below.

DISCOVERY, DAY 2

TOPIC 1	TOPIC 2
JEALOUSY	**CONTENTMENT**

1. FOCUS ON THREE SCRIPTURES.

Using a concordance, look up several Scriptures that contain topic 1. Choose three verses that seem most interesting and applicable to you. Focus on those Scriptures, writing them word-for-word in the space provided below. Choose one to study by asking the Holy Spirit to show you which verse to study today. Circle or underline it.

2. FIND THE DEFINITION.

Find and write down the Hebrew or Greek definition for topic 1.

3. FILL IN THE SCRIPTURE.

Write your chosen Scripture again and replace the word or topic with the definition you found to amplify its meaning.

4. FOLLOW THE Ps: PERUSE, PERSONALIZE, PURSUE

Peruse: Examine the details
Read the Scripture. Say it out loud. Ask God, *What do I need to know to be in this moment?*

1. Where is this taking place?

2. How does the setting bring clarity to the meaning of the verse?

3. What is happening?

4. Does the culture of that day play a role in understanding this passage? If so, how?

5. Who is speaking?

----

6. Who is the audience?

----

7. Who are the main characters, and how do they interact with others?

----

8. List any other interesting facts.

----

9. What is God's role, or how is His character shown in this story?

----

10. Summarize this Scripture passage.

Personalize: Apply the specifics
Consider how Jesus would have you apply this Scripture to your life.

Think of a time in the past when your life did not reflect this Scripture.

Confess your lack of following His Word in the past and commit to follow Christ with the truth He has shown you.

Pursue: Delight in God
True worship comes from knowing that the God of the universe placed all we need to know in the Bible because He wanted to communicate with us. He not only gave us the Bible, but He also gave us the Holy Spirit to make the Bible make sense and apply to our lives. We choose to delight in our good God. Write your words of worship to Him below.

```
DISCOVERY, DAY 3
     TOPIC 1              TOPIC 2
    JEALOUSY           CONTENTMENT
```

1. FOCUS ON THREE SCRIPTURES.

Using a concordance, look up several Scriptures that contain topic 2. Choose three verses that seem most interesting and applicable to you. Focus on those Scriptures, writing them word-for-word in the space provided below. Choose one to study by asking the Holy Spirit to show you which verse to study today. Circle or underline it.

2. FIND THE DEFINITION.

Find and write down the English definition for topic 2.

- -

3. FILL IN THE SCRIPTURE.

Write your chosen Scripture again and replace the word or topic with the definition you found to amplify its meaning.

4. FOLLOW THE Ps: PERUSE, PERSONALIZE, PURSUE

Peruse: Examine the details
Read the Scripture. Say it out loud. Ask God, *What do I need to know to be in this moment?*

1. Where is this taking place?
- -
2. How does the setting bring clarity to the meaning of the verse?
- -
3. What is happening?
- -
4. Does the culture of that day play a role in understanding this passage? If so, how?
- -
- -
- -

5. Who is speaking?

----

6. Who is the audience?

----

7. Who are the main characters, and how do they interact with others?

----

8. List any other interesting facts.

----

9. What is God's role, or how is His character shown in this story?

----

10. Summarize this Scripture passage.

Personalize: Apply the specifics

Consider how Jesus would have you apply this Scripture to your life.

Think of a time in the past when your life did not reflect this Scripture.

Confess your lack of following His Word in the past and commit to follow
Christ with the truth He has shown you.

Pursue: Delight in God

True worship comes from knowing that the God of the universe placed
all we need to know in the Bible because He wanted to communicate
with us. He not only gave us the Bible, but He also gave us the Holy Spirit
to make the Bible make sense and apply to our lives. We choose to delight
in our good God. Write your words of worship to Him below.

DISCOVERY, DAY 4

TOPIC 1	TOPIC 2
JEALOUSY	**CONTENTMENT**

1. FOCUS ON THREE SCRIPTURES.

Using a concordance, look up several Scriptures that contain topic 2. Choose three verses that seem most interesting and applicable to you. Focus on those Scriptures, writing them word-for-word in the space provided below. Choose one to study by asking the Holy Spirit to show you which verse to study today. Circle or underline it.

2. FIND THE DEFINITION.

Find and write down the Hebrew or Greek definition for topic 2.

3. FILL IN THE SCRIPTURE.

Write your chosen Scripture again and replace the word or topic with the definition you found to amplify its meaning.

4. FOLLOW THE Ps: PERUSE, PERSONALIZE, PURSUE

Peruse: Examine the details
Read the Scripture. Say it out loud. Ask God, *What do I need to know to be in this moment?*

1. Where is this taking place?

2. How does the setting bring clarity to the meaning of the verse?

3. What is happening?

4. Does the culture of that day play a role in understanding this passage? If so, how?

5. Who is speaking?

----

6. Who is the audience?

----

7. Who are the main characters, and how do they interact with others?

----

8. List any other interesting facts.

----

9. What is God's role, or how is His character shown in this story?

----

10. Summarize this Scripture passage.

Personalize: Apply the specifics
Consider how Jesus would have you apply this Scripture to your life.

Think of a time in the past when your life did not reflect this Scripture.

Confess your lack of following His Word in the past and commit to follow Christ with the truth He has shown you.

Pursue: Delight in God
True worship comes from knowing that the God of the universe placed all we need to know in the Bible because He wanted to communicate with us. He not only gave us the Bible, but He also gave us the Holy Spirit to make the Bible make sense and apply to our lives. We choose to delight in our good God. Write your words of worship to Him below.

DISCOVERY, DAY 5

TOPIC 1	TOPIC 2
JEALOUSY	**CONTENTMENT**

"At the root of covetousness [jealousy of what someone else has] is a rejection of God's sufficiency." —James MacDonald[1]

"Sisters, we need to start to clapping for one other." —Lisa Bevere[2]

PURSUE!

My favorite verse this week:

- -
- -

The definition that surprised me the most:

- -
- -

My favorite thing I learned:

- -
- -

What God showed me about His character:

- -
- -

PRAY!

• Confess that there are many times when you are jealous, wanting what someone else owns, has experienced, or has accomplished.

Ask God:
• To help you focus on what He has for you and stop coveting what others have.
• To help you celebrate victories in other people's lives, knowing God has abundant plans for you. Ask Him to strengthen you and your Sis to be brave.
• To give you the desire for the things He has already planned for you alone to do for Him and His kingdom.
• Praise God that He is the God of creativity and abundance, desiring to use and bless all of His children uniquely to impact the world.

1. James MacDonald, *Lord, Change My Attitude (Before It's Too Late)*, (Chicago: Moody Publishers, 2001), 72.
2. Lisa Bevere, *Nurture*, (New York: Faith Words, 2008), 59.

Thank God:
- That His Word is true, shedding light and wisdom into all things.
- For the uniqueness of your sister and His work in her life.

PERFORM!

(Lil Sis, it's your turn.)

Here are some suggestions for activities to highlight jealousy and contentment as you meet together:

Easy Breezy:

Arrive with earphones, a splitter, and the songs "A New Attitude" by Patti LaBelle and "Unwritten" by Natasha Bedingfield downloaded to your iPod®. Read Jeremiah 29:11 together. Turn up the tunes as you make a list of all the amazing things you would do if you thought you would never fail. Be creative. Ask God to put desires in you that match Jeremiah 29:11. Share the list with each other. Rest in this: when God starts fulfilling Jeremiah 29:11 in your life, there is no person on earth or devil below that can keep Him from bringing to pass what He has perfectly designed. Read Jeremiah 29:12-14 to discover how to find God's plan for your life.

Digging Deeper:

Meet at a your favorite coffee place. Bring four 12" ribbons in two different colors or patterns. Also bring some construction paper. Together make a bookmark for each of you. Put the words from Jeremiah 29:11 on the paper. Punch a hole in the top and tie two differently colored ribbons to it, reminding you that you two are individuals serving one purpose. Discuss how you can have an attitude of contentment so that God can fulfill Jeremiah 29:11 in your life.

Girls, dream big dreams, pray big prayers, and be confident that God will give you His best. Allow Him to put the desires of Jeremiah 29:11 in your heart. My (Mona) heart leapt today when I got an e-mail from my son Brett that perfectly wraps up this concept. It said,

"What would you do if you thought you couldn't fail? Pray your dreams to life!"

weakness vs. power

LESSON FIVE

LESSON 5: WEAKNESS VS. POWER

"I'm totally freaked about my first day of college. What if my professor makes fun of me because I'm a Christian? What if I don't make any friends? I'm not sure I'm strong enough to handle not having any friends."

"I really cannot even go to that interview. I'm straight out of college, and they require three years of experience to even submit an application. I'm not strong enough to experience the rejection of not getting this job."

"Reading the Bible is for women. I'm just a young girl. I don't need to read devotions until I'm, I don't know, like 25."

"Honestly, I cannot raise godly kids. I just started walking with the Lord a few years ago."

"To be transparent, I struggle with the same two sins. I just can't seem to shake them even though I've tried everything."

"I would love to lead a small group, but I need to wait until I'm a little stronger in my faith."

Have you ever voiced any of these or other concerns like them? Do you feel powerless in the face of everyday situations? Do you feel totally weak compared to women who have high-powered jobs, win beauty pageants, are star athletes, have straight-A kids, have probably never even said a curse word, always have perfect hair, and always say the right thing at the right time?

Considering your life yesterday, would you say you were a strong person, full of power? Did you just smile at that question, knowing you dropped your books at school or your groceries while unloading your car? Would you say you have frequent meltdowns? Or do most of your moments make others say, "Wow, she's strong"?

As women, we seem to jump into a new season of life as soon as we start to get the hang of the one we are in. Preteen life gives way to the overwhelming world of middle school. Then comes high school, college, graduation, new job, loss of job, leading a Bible study at work, getting married, having your first child, leading Bible study at church, having your child choose to go to college in Zimbabwe, and the list goes on.

Change is the only constant. You will never have one day that is identical to another. However, you can have a sure hope in a changing world. Christ is the definition of constant. Hebrews 13:8 says, "Jesus Christ is the same yesterday, today, and forever." This week you will learn how to remove lies and thoughts about weakness in your life as you meet a real, living, constant, and all-powerful God who lives in you.

> ## DISCOVERY, DAY 1
> | TOPIC 1 | TOPIC 2 |
> |---------|---------|
> | **WEAKNESS** | **POWER** |

1. FOCUS ON THREE SCRIPTURES.

Using a concordance, look up several Scriptures that contain topic 1. Choose three verses that seem most interesting and applicable to you. Focus on those Scriptures, writing them word-for-word in the space provided below. Choose one to study by asking the Holy Spirit to show you which verse to study today. Circle or underline it.

2. FIND THE DEFINITION.

Find and write down the English definition for topic 1.

3. FILL IN THE SCRIPTURE.

Write your chosen Scripture again and replace the word or topic with the definition you found to amplify its meaning.

4. FOLLOW THE Ps: PERUSE, PERSONALIZE, PURSUE

Peruse: Examine the details
Read the Scripture. Say it out loud. Ask God, *What do I need to know to be in this moment?*

1. Where is this taking place?

2. How does the setting bring clarity to the meaning of the verse?

3. What is happening?

4. Does the culture of that day play a role in understanding this passage? If so, how?

5. Who is speaking?

6. Who is the audience?

7. Who are the main characters, and how do they interact with others?

8. List any other interesting facts.

9. What is God's role, or how is His character shown in this story?

10. Summarize this Scripture passage.

Personalize: Apply the specifics
Consider how Jesus would have you apply this Scripture to your life.

Think of a time in the past when your life did not reflect this Scripture.

Confess your lack of following His Word in the past and commit to follow Christ with the truth He has shown you.

Pursue: Delight in God
True worship comes from knowing that the God of the universe placed all we need to know in the Bible because He wanted to communicate with us. He not only gave us the Bible, but He also gave us the Holy Spirit to make the Bible make sense and apply to our lives. We choose to delight in our good God. Write your words of worship to Him below.

DISCOVERY, DAY 2

TOPIC 1	TOPIC 2
WEAKNESS	**POWER**

1. FOCUS ON THREE SCRIPTURES.

Using a concordance, look up several Scriptures that contain topic 1. Choose three verses that seem most interesting and applicable to you. Focus on those Scriptures, writing them word-for-word in the space provided below. Choose one to study by asking the Holy Spirit to show you which verse to study today. Circle or underline it.

2. FIND THE DEFINITION.

Find and write down the Hebrew or Greek definition for topic 1.

3. FILL IN THE SCRIPTURE.

Write your chosen Scripture again and replace the word or topic with the definition you found to amplify its meaning.

4. FOLLOW THE Ps: PERUSE, PERSONALIZE, PURSUE

Peruse: Examine the details
Read the Scripture. Say it out loud. Ask God, *What do I need to know to be in this moment?*

1. Where is this taking place?

2. How does the setting bring clarity to the meaning of the verse?

3. What is happening?

4. Does the culture of that day play a role in understanding this passage? If so, how?

5. Who is speaking?

6. Who is the audience?

7. Who are the main characters, and how do they interact with others?

8. List any other interesting facts.

9. What is God's role, or how is His character shown in this story?

10. Summarize this Scripture passage.

Personalize: Apply the specifics
Consider how Jesus would have you apply this Scripture to your life.

Think of a time in the past when your life did not reflect this Scripture.

Confess your lack of following His Word in the past and commit to follow Christ with the truth He has shown you.

Pursue: Delight in God
True worship comes from knowing that the God of the universe placed all we need to know in the Bible because He wanted to communicate with us. He not only gave us the Bible, but He also gave us the Holy Spirit to make the Bible make sense and apply to our lives. We choose to delight in our good God. Write your words of worship to Him below.

DISCOVERY, DAY 3

TOPIC 1	TOPIC 2
WEAKNESS	**POWER**

1. FOCUS ON THREE SCRIPTURES.

Using a concordance, look up several Scriptures that contain topic 2. Choose three verses that seem most interesting and applicable to you. Focus on those Scriptures, writing them word-for-word in the space provided below. Choose one to study by asking the Holy Spirit to show you which verse to study today. Circle or underline it.

2. FIND THE DEFINITION.

Find and write down the English definition for topic 2.

3. FILL IN THE SCRIPTURE.

Write your chosen Scripture again and replace the word or topic with the definition you found to amplify its meaning.

4. FOLLOW THE Ps: PERUSE, PERSONALIZE, PURSUE

Peruse: Examine the details
Read the Scripture. Say it out loud. Ask God, *What do I need to know to be in this moment?*

1. Where is this taking place?

2. How does the setting bring clarity to the meaning of the verse?

3. What is happening?

4. Does the culture of that day play a role in understanding this passage? If so, how?

5. Who is speaking?

6. Who is the audience?

7. Who are the main characters, and how do they interact with others?

8. List any other interesting facts.

9. What is God's role, or how is His character shown in this story?

10. Summarize this Scripture passage.

Personalize: Apply the specifics

Consider how Jesus would have you apply this Scripture to your life.

Think of a time in the past when your life did not reflect this Scripture.

Confess your lack of following His Word in the past and commit to follow Christ with the truth He has shown you.

Pursue: Delight in God

True worship comes from knowing that the God of the universe placed all we need to know in the Bible because He wanted to communicate with us. He not only gave us the Bible, but He also gave us the Holy Spirit to make the Bible make sense and apply to our lives. We choose to delight in our good God. Write your words of worship to Him below.

DISCOVERY, DAY 4

TOPIC 1	TOPIC 2
WEAKNESS	**POWER**

1. FOCUS ON THREE SCRIPTURES.

Using a concordance, look up several Scriptures that contain topic 2. Choose three verses that seem most interesting and applicable to you. Focus on those Scriptures, writing them word-for-word in the space provided below. Choose one to study by asking the Holy Spirit to show you which verse to study today. Circle or underline it.

2. FIND THE DEFINITION.

Find and write down the Hebrew or Greek definition for topic 2.

3. FILL IN THE SCRIPTURE.

Write your chosen Scripture again and replace the word or topic with the definition you found to amplify its meaning.

4. FOLLOW THE Ps: PERUSE, PERSONALIZE, PURSUE

Peruse: Examine the details
Read the Scripture. Say it out loud. Ask God, *What do I need to know to be in this moment?*

1. Where is this taking place?

2. How does the setting bring clarity to the meaning of the verse?

3. What is happening?

4. Does the culture of that day play a role in understanding this passage? If so, how?

5. Who is speaking?

----

6. Who is the audience?

----

7. Who are the main characters, and how do they interact with others?

----

8. List any other interesting facts.

----

9. What is God's role, or how is His character shown in this story?

----

10. Summarize this Scripture passage.

Personalize: Apply the specifics
Consider how Jesus would have you apply this Scripture to your life.

Think of a time in the past when your life did not reflect this Scripture.

Confess your lack of following His Word in the past and commit to follow Christ with the truth He has shown you.

Pursue: Delight in God
True worship comes from knowing that the God of the universe placed all we need to know in the Bible because He wanted to communicate with us. He not only gave us the Bible, but He also gave us the Holy Spirit to make the Bible make sense and apply to our lives. We choose to delight in our good God. Write your words of worship to Him below.

DISCOVERY, DAY 5
WEAKNESS VS. POWER

"Whatever your life's work is, do it well. A man should do his job so well that the living, the dead, and the unborn could do it no better."
—Martin Luther King Jr.

"Nebuchadnezzar then approached the door of the furnace of blazing fire and called, 'Shadrach, Meshach, and Abednego, you servants of the Most High God—come out!' So Shadrach, Meshach, and Abednego came out of the fire. When the satraps, prefects, governors, and the king's advisers gathered around, they saw that the fire had no effect on the bodies of these men: not a hair of their heads was singed, their robes were unaffected, and there was no smell of fire on them." —Daniel 3:26-27

PURSUE!

My favorite verse this week:

The definition that surprised me the most:

My favorite thing I learned:

What God showed me about His character:

PRAY!

- Confess that you rely on your own strength and ability instead of recognizing that everything good comes from God.
- Ask God to forgive you for trusting yourself to provide.
- Praise God that He is your provision. He can't help but provide; provision is a part of His character.
- Thank God that He always has your best interests at heart.
- Ask God to help you to trust Him so His strength can be clearly seen in your life.

PERFORM!

(Big Sis, it's your turn.) Here are some suggestions for activities to highlight weakness and power as you meet together:

Easy Breezy: Go to The Voice of the Martyrs Web site (*www.persecution. com*) and read several stories of modern-day people who are powerful in the eyes of believers and in the sight of God, but weak in the eyes of the governments and religions that oppress them. Discuss why the world's view of strength is different than the Bible's.

Digging Deeper: Make sure you ask your sis if she has a full hour for this time together. Download the podcast from Francis Chan, "God is Strong, Am I?"[1] Get a headphone splitter and go for a walk together as you both listen to this podcast. Pick a nice trail or park if the weather is pretty. You and your sis will love this change of pace and being outdoors, hearing about God's strength in the beauty of His creation. To end your time together, make a commitment to walk in God's unlimited power, not your limited strength. We cannot control our everyday lives, but we can control whom we allow to guide us.

Final Thoughts: What place does weakness have in the life of the believer? Paul says that we should boast in our weakness. Let's think back to our intro statements. One girl said, "Reading the Bible is for women. I'm just a young girl. I don't need to read devotions until I'm, I don't know, like 25." Should she boast and be proud about this weakness? No. This weakness shows that she is relying on herself and her ability.

The kind of weakness you can be proud of is the kind that says, "God is strong, and I trust Him so much that I will not be discouraged or try to fix my own problem. I will draw my power from His unlimited strength."

See the difference? One view is that strength is found in you. The correct view is that God is power. Pure, true strength is found in Him and can be found in you when you abide in Him. Choose to trust Christ and believe that His strength is made perfect in you because of His grace and strength.

1. Francis Chan, "God is Strong, Am I?," Cornerstone Church, Simi Valley, Calif. (podcast), 10 May 2009. Available from the Internet: *http://www.cornerstonesimi. com/special/media_player.html.*

"But He said to me, 'My grace is sufficient for you, for power is perfected in weakness.' Therefore, I will most gladly boast all the more about my weaknesses, so that Christ's power may reside in me. So because of Christ, I am pleased in weaknesses, in insults, in catastrophes, in persecutions, and in pressures. For when I am weak, then I am strong."
—2 Corinthians 12:9-10

bitterness vs. forgiveness

LESSON SIX

LESSON 6: BITTERNESS VS. FORGIVENESS

Sour Patch® candies—what an oxymoron. Candy is supposed to be sweet, not sour. Sour is for pickles. Yet these candies are an international favorite. From cute little bears to long strings, the one constant is the deceptive sugar coating on the outside. It looks so sweet and inviting. Until you sink your teeth in and find what it's really made of—super sour stuff that will have your saliva glands rebelling.

Let me expound on the correlation between this little candy and our topic of bitterness. Think about how'd you'd react in the following situations:

• Your significant other lied to or cheated on you, leaving you feeling rejected and unloved.

• Your best friend gossiped about your deepest secret on Facebook. You're hurt and embarrassed.

• A store clerk refused to allow you to return a shirt that had a stain, insisting you caused the stain. Injustice and anger filled you.

The stories may differ, but everyone at all stages of life comes in contact with situations that are less than sweet, leaving them feeling bitter and angry. What's a girl to do?

When someone hurts us, we need to pause for a minute and understand that the next move is ours. We get to decide whether we will choose to forgive or choose to be bitter, keeping the sourness of it all hidden deep inside as we smile sugarcoated smiles at the world, justifying ourselves with thoughts like, "I am right," "It isn't fair," "You don't know what they did to me," or "I'm perfectly fine."

Those statements might even be valid. But we cannot be fooled by the lie that it is OK to stay bitter and angry. Jesus was very clear about forgiveness. By acting sweet to the outside world even though we are sour and bitter on the inside, we end up deceiving ourselves as well as others.

Did you know that one of the last things Jesus talked about on the cross was forgiveness? And it was one of the first things He talked about after His resurrection. God is in the forgiveness business. His mercy and grace toward us are always available. Salvation through Jesus' sacrifice on the cross provides total forgiveness for all we have done or will do wrong.

We humans have a little harder time putting the forgiveness thing into action. But we can do it. Take time to read Matthew 18:21-35 this week. Isn't it amazing that someone who had been forgiven of so much could refuse to forgive someone for something so small? God's Word is the best place to get an accurate understanding of true forgiveness.

When I told a friend about my Sour Patch® analogy, she laughed. "Mona, you may not know this, but if you keep working at the candy in your mouth, the bitterness comes off, and all you are left with is super sweetness." I always spit the thing out. But, thanks to a friend who pointed out what I need to do, I now can complete my analogy.

Don't give up. Work through the bitterness, even if you hate it and want to get rid of the whole thing. Allow God to wash the bitterness away and replace it with the sweet satisfaction of forgiveness. Oh, and listening to a sister's point of view always adds extra flavor.

This week you will be working on removing bitterness and replacing it with forgiveness. These topics are serious, deep, and life-changing. I strongly urge you to allow the Holy Spirit to lead you. You can read a lot of books about forgiveness, but the best book is the Bible. Trust me—the freedom and joy you will experience will be worth the work. As you head into this sweet-and-sour subject, let me give you a few forgiveness facts to assist you:

- Forgiveness does not mean you agree with the other person or that what they did was right. Jesus forgave us while knowing what we did (or would do) was wrong. (See Isa. 1:18.)
- Forgiveness does not mean you have to go back into relationship with the person. Jesus offers forgiveness to the world; however, the whole world is not reconciled back into relationship with Him. (See John 3:16.)
- Bitterness will affect every fruit that comes from your life (Acts 8:22-23).
- Bitterness is like a poison to your mind, your body, and your joy, hurting only you (Prov. 14:10).
- God wants to help. In fact, He is the only One who can (Ps. 46:1).

And if you were drooling through this whole section and are now eating Sour Patch® candy, get those sticky fingers cleaned up before heading into your study!

DISCOVERY, DAY 1

TOPIC 1	TOPIC 2
BITTERNESS	**FORGIVENESS**

1. FOCUS ON THREE SCRIPTURES.

Using a concordance, look up several Scriptures that contain topic 1. Choose three verses that seem most interesting and applicable to you. Focus on those Scriptures, writing them word-for-word in the space provided below. Choose one to study by asking the Holy Spirit to show you which verse to study today. Circle or underline it.

2. FIND THE DEFINITION.

Find and write down the English definition for topic 1.

3. FILL IN THE SCRIPTURE.

Write your chosen Scripture again and replace the word or topic with the definition you found to amplify its meaning.

4. FOLLOW THE Ps: PERUSE, PERSONALIZE, PURSUE

Peruse: Examine the details

Read the Scripture. Say it out loud. Ask God, *What do I need to know to be in this moment?*

1. Where is this taking place?

2. How does the setting bring clarity to the meaning of the verse?

3. What is happening?

4. Does the culture of that day play a role in understanding this passage? If so, how?

5. Who is speaking?

- -

6. Who is the audience?

- -

7. Who are the main characters, and how do they interact with others?

- -

- -

8. List any other interesting facts.

- -

- -

9. What is God's role, or how is His character shown in this story?

- -

10. Summarize this Scripture passage.

- -

- -

- -

- -

Personalize: Apply the specifics
Consider how Jesus would have you apply this Scripture to your life.

- -

- -

Think of a time in the past when your life did not reflect this Scripture.

- -

- -

Confess your lack of following His Word in the past and commit to follow Christ with the truth He has shown you.

- -

- -

Pursue: Delight in God
True worship comes from knowing that the God of the universe placed all we need to know in the Bible because He wanted to communicate with us. He not only gave us the Bible, but He also gave us the Holy Spirit to make the Bible make sense and apply to our lives. We choose to delight in our good God. Write your words of worship to Him below.

- -

- -

- -

- -

DISCOVERY, DAY 2

TOPIC 1	TOPIC 2
BITTERNESS	**FORGIVENESS**

1. FOCUS ON THREE SCRIPTURES.

Using a concordance, look up several Scriptures that contain topic 1. Choose three verses that seem most interesting and applicable to you. Focus on those Scriptures, writing them word-for-word in the space provided below. Choose one to study by asking the Holy Spirit to show you which verse to study today. Circle or underline it.

2. FIND THE DEFINITION.

Find and write down the Hebrew or Greek definition for topic 1.

3. FILL IN THE SCRIPTURE.

Write your chosen Scripture again and replace the word or topic with the definition you found to amplify its meaning.

4. FOLLOW THE Ps: PERUSE, PERSONALIZE, PURSUE

Peruse: Examine the details

Read the Scripture. Say it out loud. Ask God, *What do I need to know to be in this moment?*

1. Where is this taking place?

2. How does the setting bring clarity to the meaning of the verse?

3. What is happening?

4. Does the culture of that day play a role in understanding this passage? If so, how?

5. Who is speaking?

------

6. Who is the audience?

------

7. Who are the main characters, and how do they interact with others?

------

8. List any other interesting facts.

------

9. What is God's role, or how is His character shown in this story?

------

10. Summarize this Scripture passage.

Personalize: Apply the specifics

Consider how Jesus would have you apply this Scripture to your life.

Think of a time in the past when your life did not reflect this Scripture.

Confess your lack of following His Word in the past and commit to follow Christ with the truth He has shown you.

Pursue: Delight in God

True worship comes from knowing that the God of the universe placed all we need to know in the Bible because He wanted to communicate with us. He not only gave us the Bible, but He also gave us the Holy Spirit to make the Bible make sense and apply to our lives. We choose to delight in our good God. Write your words of worship to Him below.

DISCOVERY, DAY 3

TOPIC 1	TOPIC 2
BITTERNESS	**FORGIVENESS**

1. FOCUS ON THREE SCRIPTURES.

Using a concordance, look up several Scriptures that contain topic 2. Choose three verses that seem most interesting and applicable to you. Focus on those Scriptures, writing them word-for-word in the space provided below. Choose one to study by asking the Holy Spirit to show you which verse to study today. Circle or underline it.

2. FIND THE DEFINITION.

Find and write down the English definition for topic 2.

3. FILL IN THE SCRIPTURE.

Write your chosen Scripture again and replace the word or topic with the definition you found to amplify its meaning.

4. FOLLOW THE Ps: PERUSE, PERSONALIZE, PURSUE

Peruse: Examine the details

Read the Scripture. Say it out loud. Ask God, *What do I need to know to be in this moment?*

1. Where is this taking place?

2. How does the setting bring clarity to the meaning of the verse?

3. What is happening?

4. Does the culture of that day play a role in understanding this passage? If so, how?

5. Who is speaking?

----

6. Who is the audience?

----

7. Who are the main characters, and how do they interact with others?

----

8. List any other interesting facts.

----

9. What is God's role, or how is His character shown in this story?

----

10. Summarize this Scripture passage.

Personalize: Apply the specifics

Consider how Jesus would have you apply this Scripture to your life.

Think of a time in the past when your life did not reflect this Scripture.

Confess your lack of following His Word in the past and commit to follow
Christ with the truth He has shown you.

Pursue: Delight in God

True worship comes from knowing that the God of the universe placed
all we need to know in the Bible because He wanted to communicate
with us. He not only gave us the Bible, but He also gave us the Holy Spirit
to make the Bible make sense and apply to our lives. We choose to delight
in our good God. Write your words of worship to Him below.

> ### DISCOVERY, DAY 4
> TOPIC 1   TOPIC 2
> **BITTERNESS**   **FORGIVENESS**

1. FOCUS ON THREE SCRIPTURES.

Using a concordance, look up several Scriptures that contain topic 2. Choose three verses that seem most interesting and applicable to you. Focus on those Scriptures, writing them word-for-word in the space provided below. Choose one to study by asking the Holy Spirit to show you which verse to study today. Circle or underline it.

2. FIND THE DEFINITION.

Find and write down the Hebrew or Greek definition for topic 2.

- -

3. FILL IN THE SCRIPTURE.

Write your chosen Scripture again and replace the word or topic with the definition you found to amplify its meaning.

4. FOLLOW THE Ps: PERUSE, PERSONALIZE, PURSUE

Peruse: Examine the details

Read the Scripture. Say it out loud. Ask God, *What do I need to know to be in this moment?*

1. Where is this taking place?

- -

2. How does the setting bring clarity to the meaning of the verse?

- -

3. What is happening?

- -

4. Does the culture of that day play a role in understanding this passage? If so, how?

- -

- -

- -

5. Who is speaking?

----

6. Who is the audience?

----

7. Who are the main characters, and how do they interact with others?

----

8. List any other interesting facts.

----

9. What is God's role, or how is His character shown in this story?

----

10. Summarize this Scripture passage.

Personalize: Apply the specifics

Consider how Jesus would have you apply this Scripture to your life.

Think of a time in the past when your life did not reflect this Scripture.

Confess your lack of following His Word in the past and commit to follow Christ with the truth He has shown you.

Pursue: Delight in God

True worship comes from knowing that the God of the universe placed all we need to know in the Bible because He wanted to communicate with us. He not only gave us the Bible, but He also gave us the Holy Spirit to make the Bible make sense and apply to our lives. We choose to delight in our good God. Write your words of worship to Him below.

> ### DISCOVERY, DAY 5
> | TOPIC 1 | TOPIC 2 |
> |---------|---------|
> | **BITTERNESS** | **FORGIVENESS** |

"Bitterness is like drinking poison and hoping the other person will die."
—*Unknown*

"It is highly displeasing to God for you not to forgive yourself, and it is highly pleasing to Satan when you do not forgive yourself. Do you want to please the devil? I don't think so!" —*R.T. Kendall*[1]

PURSUE!
My favorite verse this week:

The definition that surprised me the most:

My favorite thing I learned:

What God showed me about His character:

PRAY!
• Confess any unforgiveness you have toward others including yourself. Ask God:
• To show you where you are wounded and where bitterness is hiding.
• To heal you of your pain and allow you to forgive.

Thank God:
• For the truth that sets you free.
• For His love and forgiveness toward you.

PERFORM!
(Lil Sis, it's your turn.)
Here are some suggestions for activities to highlight bitterness and forgiveness as you meet together:

1. R.T. Kendall, *How to Forgive Ourselves—Totally*, (Lake Mary, FL: Charisma House, 2007), 49-59.

Easy Breezy: OK, you saw this one coming. Get several different kinds of sour candy and share it with your sis when you meet. Discuss areas where you each hide behind sugarcoated smiles when underneath you are sour and bitter. Agree to hold one another accountable for working through the struggle. Choose several Scriptures to text each other every day this week as encouragement. Forgiveness is serious business and worth every bit of the effort.

Digging Deeper: Meet at a church or private place for this week's time together. Before arriving, have a list of people and situations that need your forgiveness. Please consider that you may have to place yourself on that list. We must forgive ourselves for failures. Talk to your sis about your week in God's Word. Then spend some time alone with God and your list. Go to God in prayer and ask Him to help you forgive.

Possible steps for your forgiveness prayer time:
- Ask the Holy Spirit to calm your emotions and help you understand what caused the bitterness.
- Rethink the offense. Don't let your emotions get you side-tracked.
- Identify the root pain you felt (like feeling unloved, rejected, or angry).
- Consider how Jesus and the Word could remove the lie and replace it with truth that will heal you.
- Ask Jesus to help you forgive the person. It might help to see the person or situation in your mind's eye.
- Tell the person you forgive him or her because Jesus forgave you. Knowing that Jesus is taking care of you will allow you to let Jesus handle that person.
- Let God remove the bitterness and unforgiveness from your heart.
- Thank and praise Jesus for what He alone can be and do for you.

This is an important topic. We suggest reading *Total Forgiveness* and *How to Forgive Ourselves—Totally*, both by R.T. Kendall.

Two Ways to Earn Credit
for Studying LifeWay Christian Resources Material

CHRISTIAN GROWTH STUDY PLAN

CONTACT INFORMATION:
Christian Growth Study Plan
One LifeWay Plaza, MSN 117
Nashville, TN 37234
CGSP info line 1-800-968-5519
www.lifeway.com/CGSP
To order resources 1-800-485-2772

Christian Growth Study Plan resources are available for course credit for personal growth and church leadership training.

Courses are designed as plans for personal spiritual growth and for training current and future church leaders. To receive credit, complete the book, material, or activity. Respond to the learning activities or attend group sessions, when applicable, and show your work to your pastor, staff member, or church leader. Then go to *www.lifeway.com/CGSP*, or call the toll-free number for instructions for receiving credit and your certificate of completion.

For information about studies in the Christian Growth Study Plan, refer to the current catalog online at the CGSP Web address. This program and certificate are free LifeWay services to you.

Need a CEU?

CONTACT INFORMATION:
CEU Coordinator
One LifeWay Plaza, MSN 150
Nashville, TN 37234
Info line 1-800-968-5519
www.lifeway.com/CEU

Receive Continuing Education Units (CEUs) when you complete group Bible studies by your favorite LifeWay authors.

Some studies are approved by the Association of Christian Schools International (ACSI) for CEU credits. Do you need to renew your Christian school teaching certificate? Gather a group of teachers or neighbors and complete one of the approved studies. Then go to *www.lifeway.com/CEU* to submit a request form or to find a list of ACSI-approved LifeWay studies and conferences. Book studies must be completed in a group setting. Online courses approved for ACSI credit are also noted on the course list. The administrative cost of each CEU certificate is only $10 per course.